Aikido
WEAPONS TECHNIQUES

The Wooden Sword, Stick, and Knife of Aikido

SENSEI PHONG THONG DANG
Sixth-Degree Aikido Black Belt
Founder of the International Tenshinkai Aikido Federation
Two-Time Inductee into the World Martial Arts Hall of Fame
Chief Instructor, Westminster Aikikai Dojo

LYNN SEISER, Ph.D.
Third-Degree Aikido Black Belt
Founder of Aiki-Solutions

TUTTLE PUBLISHING
Tokyo · Rutland, Vermont · Singapore

Please note that the publisher and authors of this instructional book are NOT RESPONSIBLE in any manner whatsoever for any injury that may result from practicing the techniques and/or following the instructions given within. Martial arts training can be dangerous—both to you and to others—if not practiced safely. If you're in doubt as to how to proceed or whether your practice is safe, consult with a trained martial arts teacher before beginning. Since the physical activities described herein may be too strenuous in nature for some readers, it is also essential that a physician be consulted prior to training.

Published by Tuttle Publishing, an imprint of Periplus Editions (HK) Ltd., with editorial offices at 364 Innovation Drive, North Clarendon, Vermont 05759 U.S.A.

Library of Congress Cataloging-in-Publication Data
Dang, Phong Thong, 1940–
Aikido weapons techniques : the wooden sword, stick, and knife of
aikido / Sensei Phong Thong Dang, Lynn Seiser.
      p. cm.
Includes bibliographical references.
ISBN 0-8048-3641-8 (pbk. : alk. paper)
1. Aikido. I. Seiser, Lynn, 1950– II. Title.
GV1114.35.D376 2006
796.6—dc22
                                        2006001500
ISBN-10: 0-8048-3641-8
ISBN-13: 978-0-8048-3641-8

Distributed by

North America, Latin America &
Europe
Tuttle Publishing
364 Innovation Drive
North Clarendon, VT 05759-9436 U.S.A.
Tel: (1) 802 773-8930
Fax: (1) 802 773-6993
info@tuttlepublishing.com
www.tuttlepublishing.com

Asia Pacific
Berkeley Books Pte. Ltd.
130 Joo Seng Road #06-01
Singapore 368357
Tel: (65) 6280-1330
Fax: (65) 6280-6290
inquiries@periplus.com.sg
www.periplus.com

First edition
10 09 08 07 06   10 9 8 7 6 5 4 3 2 1

Printed in the United States of America

TUTTLE PUBLISHING® is a registered trademark of Tuttle Publishing, a division of Periplus Editions (Hk) Ltd.

DEDICATION

I would like to dedicate this book to the founder of aikido, O'Sensei Morihei Ueshiba; his son, Kisshomaru Ueshiba; and his grandson, the current Doshu Moriteru Ueshiba. I want to thank the Aikikai Foundation, and Secretary General Shihan Masatake Fujita for his ongoing support and encouragement. I also dedicate this work to my first aikido instructor, Shihan Mutsuro Nakazono, and my late brother, Sensei Tri Thong Dang.

I dedicate this book, and my life's work, to my students.

As always, I dedicate this book to my loving and patient family.

—Sensei Phong Thong Dang

As always, first I must dedicate this book, our third together, with my deepest respect and humility, to my aikido sensei, Phong Thong Dang. His technical precision and expertise are exceptional. His patience with his students demonstrates and illustrates a deep compassion and desire to communicate and perpetuate his life's work and the shared passion and vision of aikido founder O'Sensei Morihei Ueshiba. It is truly a humbling honor to train under such a man, a legend in martial arts, to share in his vision and be entrusted with assisting in presenting this knowledge, as limited as my understanding may be and as inadequate as my words are. *"Sensei, Domo Arigato Gozaimashita."*

I dedicate this work to all the people I have ever had the honor and pleasure to train with. The hours we have spent in sweat and in laughter have contributed greatly to this work and to my life. What they have given me freely I have tried to pass on as freely and completely as it was given. I hope that in some small way these works will help those training partners I will never meet but who share a similar journey.

I dedicate this work, my love, and my life, to my family. Their patience, encouragement, and support make my training possible, my dreams come true, and my life worthwhile. With them in my heart and mind, my training is always an art and discipline of loving protection.

—Lynn Seiser, Ph.D.

CONTENTS

ACKNOWLEDGMENTS AND APPRECIATION

The authors express their deepest acknowledgments, appreciation, and gratitude to their editor, Jennifer Brown, at Tuttle Publishing, for her patience, support, encouragement, and expertise. Without her, our two previous volumes would not have been possible. It is hard to transform men of action into men of words. The authors also want to express their appreciation to Amanda Dupuis for her guidance, assistance, and patience with this, our third volume.

John Tran, of the Westminster Aikikai Dojo, took the photographs used in this book. His patience, and his knowing eye for technique, are acknowledged and deeply appreciated.

The models used in this book, along with Sensei Phong Thong Dang, were Westminster Aikikai students Minhhai Nguyen, Bryan Tate, and Richmond Neff. The task of receiving a technique and taking a fall is difficult and often dangerous. Without good training partners, there is no aikido training or practice. These gentlemen are some of the best.

Pamela Seiser, wife of Lynn Seiser, has read, reread, and proofread every word, of every page, of every draft, of every book. Her eye for spelling, grammar, style, and general readability has been an invaluable service to the authors, the editor, and those of you who read these works. Her support and encouragement made these works possible. Her expertise and eye for detail have made them presentable.

Lynn Seiser painted the original *kanji* calligraphy for each chapter.

INTRODUCTION

The history of the world is often told by the history of war, recorded by the victor. Warriors have always used weapons to fight wars, and any complete fighting system includes the use of weapons. While aikido is an effective and efficient means of self-defense and protection—popularly practiced primarily as a means of personal, social, and spiritual development—it is still, at its core, a martial art.

Japanese Weapon Arts

The mystique of the use of Japanese weapons appears in the *Kojiki* or legendary stories of old Japan. The Japanese feudal warrior was called *bushi*, but later commonly became known as *samurai* (meaning "to serve"), in the Muromachi period (1392–1573). The bushi's trade was *bugei,* or martial arts. Bugei, combative effective martial art systems, were known by the *jutsu* suffix. They developed systematically from around the tenth century, through vigorous traditional training discipline, for the sole purpose of group protection. The martial arts included both unarmed and armed fighting arts, as well as arts of camouflage and deception, binding, speed walking and running, jumping, climbing, dodging, swimming, fortification, deployment, gunnery, and fire. Within those armed or weapons martial arts were *kyu-jutsu* (bow and arrow), *so-jutsu* (spear), *gekikan-jutsu* (ball and chain), *shuriken-jutsu* (blade throwing), *jutte-jutsu* (metal truncheon), *tessen-jutsu* (iron fan), *tetsubo-jutsu* (iron bar), *sodegarami-jutsu* (barbed pole), *sasu-mata-jutsu* (forked staff), and *juken-jutsu* (bayonet). The more common weapons were *ken-jutsu* (offensive swordsmanship), *iai-jutsu* (defensive swordsmanship), *bo-jutsu* (staff over five feet long), and jo-jutsu (staff or stick under five feet long). (Draeger and Smith 1969, p. 83)

The bushi's moral code of ethics, moral standards, philosophy, and national consciousness was *bushido,* "the way of the warrior." Many recognize three ages of bushido: ancient martial bushido of the eleventh century, reformed bushido of the seventeenth century, and modern bushido of the nineteenth century (Random 1977, pp. 36–37). The essence of bushido lay in justice, courage, benevolence, politeness, honesty, honor, and loyalty (Draeger and Smith 1969, pp. 88–89). The role of the samurai is tied to the core concept of *giri,* or duty. To be of service to his lord, the samurai followed the duty and obligation of his status and training by being the best warrior, soldier, bodyguard, and protector possible. The eleven volumes of *Hagakure,* completed in 1716, are a classic in bushido. The presence and acceptance of death was a central theme. Although idealized and romanticized, the life of the samurai was one of self-sacrifice, loneliness, danger, and inevitably death (with honor, it was hoped).

The way of life of a bushi was to be a warrior and fight wars. Later, the way of life of a samurai was to be of service in other ways as well. Both

O'Sensei Morihei Ueshiba embodied the true spirit of budo with the traditional values, ethics, and social responsibilities of a warrior.

O'Sensei Morihei Ueshiba in a traditional portrait often seen on the front shomen of a dojo, honoring his gift of aikido.

periods and ways of life followed the guidelines of bushido and became known as *budo*. The *do* arts evolved from the jutsu systems, beginning in the eighteenth century. They were concerned with the "higher aims," spiritual discipline and both mental and physical self-perfection (Draeger and Smith 1969, pp. 90–91). Jutsu arts are effective and efficient practical application systems of fighting and combat. Do arts are oriented toward personal and spiritual development through physical training. *Aiki-jujitsu* evolved into aikido. Ken-jutsu and iai-jutsu evolved into *iai-do, kendo,* and *aiki-ken*. Jo-jutsu evolved into *aiki-jo*. Aikido is a modern art in the true traditional budo sense.

It can be said that aikido *buki-waza*, or weapons techniques, comes from "empty-hand" techniques, and that empty-hand techniques come from weapons. The two, though often thought of as very different, are very much an interrelated and interdependent extension of each other. No empty-hand system is complete without weapons training, and no weapons system is complete without knowing how to fight with empty hands.

The Introduction of Weapons to Aikido

Aikido is a modern nonviolent, noncompetitive martial art. It places an emphasis on personal, social, and spiritual development, while preserving traditional values and appearance. Aikido also provides efficient and effective self-defense skills. Aikido is the way to harmonize with the energy or spirit of the universe.

Initially, aikido appears to be a martial art of throwing opponents by utilizing the momentum of the attack. Most techniques are done from a *tachi-waza* (standing) or *suwari-waza* (kneeling) position. The *nage-waza* (throwing techniques) of aikido are dynamic and appear effortless. The *katame-waza* (joint lock, pinning or immobilization techniques) of aikido are painful and demand cooperation, compliance, and submission. Unfortunately, seldom does one see the buki-waza (wooden weapon techniques) of aikido taught or demonstrated. The wooden weapons apply and illustrate the same technical proficiency, the same sequential applications, and the same conceptual orientation as the empty-hand techniques. Anything that can be done with the empty hand can be done with the wooden weapon.

O'Sensei Morihei Ueshiba (1883–1969), the founder of aikido, personally trained and practiced with the wooden weapons. He was known to go off into the night and train, being taught by the *kamisama* (spirits). He watched other schools, styles, or systems train with weapons and then added his own unique concepts and movements to make them into the aikido way. Although it would be unfair and inaccurate to state that aikido uses the wooden weapons in the same way as these other schools, it can be said that the other schools, styles, and systems studied and observed by O'Sensei Morihei Ueshiba influenced his unique adaptation of the wooden weapon. In aikido, the wooden weapons are used to execute techniques and illustrate concepts; they are not seen as separate from the main body of concepts and techniques of aikido.

While developing the art of aikido, O'Sensei Morihei Ueshiba investigated and studied approximately two hundred martial arts or jutsu systems. *Daito-ryu* aiki-jujitsu is acknowledged as the foundation for many of aikido's unarmed physical techniques. Takeda Sensei (1859–1943), the founder of this art, was a master swordsman and weapons expert who studied many different fighting systems. Daito-ryu aiki-jujitsu techniques, though similar in appearance, are not the same as the physical techniques of aikido, due to O'Sensei Morihei Ueshiba's application of *taisabaki* (body turning), *irimi* (entering), and *awase* (blending); his application and extension of ki; and his emphasis and focus on spiritual and personal development, over martial, combative, or fighting effectiveness and efficiency. O'Sensei Morihei Ueshiba thanked Takeda Sensei and credited him with introducing him to true budo. He frequently stated that aikido is based on the sword.

O'Sensei Morihei Ueshiba also studied *Yagyo* ken-jutsu, *Hozoin* so-jutsu (spear), and especially *Kashima Shinto-ryu* ken-jutsu (which was an offshoot of *Katori Shinto-ryu*). It was to this later school of swordsmanship that O'Sensei Morihei Ueshiba took a blood oath in 1937. His second son, Kisshomaru Ueshiba (1921–1999), who later became the first Doshu, also had extensive training in Kashima Shinto-ryu ken-jutsu. O'Sensei Morihei Ueshiba would watch his son train in the technique and then adapt it to the aiki way.

Doshu Kisshomaru Ueshiba demonstrates proper execution and extension to throw an opponent using the jo.

Although aikido has these roots in weapons training, many highly skilled aikido practitioners spend little or no time training directly with the wooden weapons. Many feel that in a modern world, training with a wooden stick or sword is antiquated and useless. Aikido founder O'Sensei Morihei Ueshiba did not encourage weapons training at his aikido school, known as the Hombu Dojo. *Hombu Dojo* means the "home," "headquarters," or "main school" of training. Currently the Hombu Dojo, established by O'Sensei in Tokyo, Japan, and dedicated in January 1968 for the Aikikai Foundation, perpetuates his techniques, training, and vision of aikido. Therefore, there is no "Hombu" style of wooden weapons fighting. Trainees, in the early days at the Hombu Dojo, would attend special classes or seminars, or take private lessons. Others would just naturally begin to experiment with the wooden weapons themselves. Many felt the wooden weapons to be secondary to empty-hand techniques. The goal was to use wooden weapons to illustrate principles and movements and to train aikido techniques against them, rather than actually to have a separate and specific style of weapons fighting. However, O'Sensei Morihei Ueshiba did support the weapons training at the Iwama Dojo under Saito Sensei (1928–2002). It was here that aikido wooden weapons training became known as *Iwama-ryu* or aiki-ken and aiki-jo, as a somewhat distinct style.

About This Book

The aikido practitioner uses the wooden weapons for personal, social, and spiritual development as well as to defeat an enemy and protect loved ones. Aikido techniques that use the wooden weapons illustrate basic and advanced aikido technical tactics as well as sequential and conceptual strategies and skills.

This book focuses on the wooden *ken, jo,* and *tanto.* These weapons are usually made of red (less expensive) or white oak because it will not crack, crush, or splinter on impact with other weapons. Your wooden weapon should have a straight tight grain, be properly seasoned, and be without warp.

The ken is traditionally forty-one inches in length and of varied weights, according to individual preference. The jo is traditionally between fifty and one-half inches and fifty-four inches in length, but can be as long as fifty-six inches. It is one-half inch to one inch in diameter and of varied weights, according to individual preference. The practical rule for jo length is from the ground to the armpit.

Wooden weapons should be stored by laying them horizontally flat on the floor or in a rack to prevent warping. They should be carried in a protective weapons case to prevent damage from moisture or sunlight, and for convenience. Periodic cleaning and maintenance of the wooden weapons require a light coating with tung or linseed oil, rubbed in with steel wool, following the grain of the wood.

This work does not present ken-jutsu or kendo, iai-jutsu or iai-do sword techniques. There are other, more authoritative books for that grand task. This work will not present the wooden weapons of aikido founder O'Sensei Morihei Ueshiba, for only he can do that. This work will not present the aiki-jo or aiki-ken of Saito Sensei, of the Iwama Dojo, who has done a brilliant job of preserving the movements taught to him directly by O'Sensei Morihei Ueshiba.

What this work presents, illustrates, demonstrates, and describes is some of the aikido concepts, training, and techniques expressed through wooden weapons in accordance with the understanding and interpretation of Sensei Phong Thong Dang. Phong Sensei is the founder of the International Tenshinkai Aikido Federation, a sixth dan in aikikai aikido, and a two-time inductee into the World Martial Arts Hall of Fame. The wooden weapons techniques included in this work are conceptually influenced by, and congruent with, the aikikai weapons practices of O'Sensei Morihei Ueshiba and the aiki-ken and aiki-jo of Saito Sensei's Iwama-ryu.

While one picture can communicate more than a thousand words, action will always communicate more than a thousand pictures. No words or pictures can express or replace action. No words or pictures in a book can teach someone how to effectively and efficiently utilize and apply the technical, sequential, and conceptual principles of aikido to the wooden weapon. Words and pictures can, however, be useful reminders and guides of what one learns under the competent instruction, observation, and supervision of a skilled and competent aikido sensei.

Chapter 1

KIHON: BASICS AND FUNDAMENTALS

Before we discuss the fundamentals of weapons practice, this chapter will provide an overview of concepts and theories basic to aikido. Although you should already be familiar with these ideas, it's important to rethink them for practice with weapons.

Rei: Etiquette

Everything in aikido starts and ends with the bow. Showing respect to all beings, and toward everything one does, must become an attitude to life in general. Mutual respect, appreciation, and protection are the cornerstones of aikido training. Over time, the attribute of etiquette is generalized and applied effectively and efficiently in any conflict situation. It is surprising how many conflicts are prevented, managed, or resolved using a sense of humor, humility, and good manners.

O'Sensei Morihei Ueshiba trains in technical execution of the jo with his son, second Doshu Kisshomaru Ueshiba.

Technical Execution

Nonresistance is an essential element of proper aikido technique execution. Intercepting, deflecting, and redirecting an attack—rather than blocking or resisting it—utilize the momentum and inertia of the attack. This is initially practiced by training to get off the line of attack, and by not attempting to stop an attack with force. Nonresistance does not mean being passively overpowered by the attack; that is a fear-based response that perpetuates a win-lose dynamic counter to the basic tenets of aikido. Nonresistance is the positive and active entering, joining, and blending with an attack; the goal is a mutually beneficial win-win conclusion in which no one, including the attacker, gets hurt in any way. Rather than blocking an attack, an aikido practitioner with a weapon will simply avoid the strike, allowing it to follow its course without interruption, and then intercept the hands or body as the target. Just as the empty-hand techniques of aikido apply nonresistance, the same techniques can be executed with or against a weapon.

It is always important to maintain good posture and a relaxed body. Good posture increases a sense of power and self-esteem. Good posture maintains a structurally supportive skeletal system and allows for the proper functioning of the central nervous system. Good posture maintains a sense of balance, stability, and mobility. Keeping the body relaxed minimizes stress, anxiety, and fear responses, while preventing antagonistic muscles from working against fluid responsive movement. Proper posture maintains balance, which is vitally important when executing aikido techniques with or against a weapon, since the extended range and torque of a weapon require a stable base.

Like good posture, structural alignment is also very important. Structural alignment ensures that maximum support is provided horizontally and vertically by the skeletal and muscular systems of the body. Structural alignment extends into the attacker so that a simple movement of the wrist aligns and interlocks the structural system toward the attacker's *kuzushi* (balance point) and causes a loss of balance. Many aikido techniques facilitate the loss of structural alignment in the attacker, resulting in a total loss of control and power. The physical structural alignment of the body must extend beyond the body and through the tip of the weapon to maintain stability and ki energy flow.

It is important to remain aware of the centerline—the imaginary line that runs directly down the body, dividing it equally into left and right. Keeping your hands on the centerline allows you to defend with more rapidity and efficiency. Maintaining your hands on the centerline also facilitates turning or pivoting from the hips or stepping with the feet, projecting full body power, momentum, and inertia into every movement. Maintaining visual awareness of the attacker's centerline provides a larger field of vision and facilitates a greater use of peripheral vision to detect movement of both the upper and lower body. Alignment to both centerlines (yours and your attacker's) provides a connection and positioning, which adds to the effectiveness and efficiency of the technique you execute. The path of the weapon must follow the centerline of the body, especially when executing an overhead *shomen-uchi* strike. The weapon is always held in front of the body centerline, and movement is initiated by turning the whole body.

Another important line to stay aware of is the line of attack—the imaginary line that demonstrates and denotes the direction of the incoming attack. The attack line usually follows the attacker's centerline, directed through the feet, to the centerline of the defender's body. The best rule to remember is to "get off the attack line" to ensure that you are not grabbed or hit. When you get off the attack line, you will not only avoid meeting the attack with the anticipated resistance, but you will also allow the natural momentum and inertia of the attack to become overextended. The attacker will then reach beyond his range of power and lose his balance. Even a large, well-trained attacker with a weapon is easier to control when he is off balance, and is harder to hit when he is off the direct line of intended attack. It takes awareness and experience to adapt and calibrate the extended line of attack in weapons training, both offensively and defensively.

Everything in nature has a rhythm, and aikido is said to follow the laws and ways of nature. There is an internal rhythm coordinating body movement. The arms, torso, and legs move in unison, as if following the same rhythm. There is also the rhythm between practitioners. As dance partners move to the same beat, aikido practitioners also move together, to the same rhythm. This entering into and blending within the same rhythm facilitates a fluid exchange and responsiveness to techniques. Finding the rhythm of movement is important in weapons training. All movement initiates, avoids, or even interrupts the rhythm. In the dojo, the sound of wood against wood makes the rhythm of weapons training obvious and exciting.

Timing is more important than speed. Timing is that inexpressible magic of being in just the right place, at just the right time, to let just the right thing happen. If one gets to the point too soon or too late, the magic does not happen. The smooth, fluid execution of aikido technique is a result of the impeccable timing that blends attacker and defender into one fluid motion, much like notes in a melody blending to form a beautiful harmony. The extended distance of a weapon attack and the danger of miscalculation make timing extremely important in weapons training.

The center is different from the centerline. While the centerline contains the center, the center is but one point (perhaps the most important point) on the centerline. The center is very important in aikido. One must maintain one's own center and move from it. One must also become the center of the technique and assist the attacker in losing his center of balance. The center is the imaginary, yet actual, center of the body. That point, halfway between top and bottom, left and right, front and back, is the center. It is located in the hip region slightly below navel level. Many assert that maintaining awareness in the center will make for a powerful and "centered" technique and life. In weapons training, the weapon extends in front of the center. As in empty-hand training, all aikido weapons techniques move from the center and allow awareness to settle there.

Contact can be initiated, intercepted, or focused on the attacker's intent. Initiating contact and intercepting the momentum and inertia of any attack—with the empty hand or a wooden weapon—can take place at several different references to space and time. *Sen* is the initiative taken after an opponent's position is analyzed. *Gono-sen* means immediately counterattacking. *Sen-no-sen* is taking the initiative and intercepting or counterattacking the opponent's attack before the opponent has physically initiated it. Ultimately, this depends on subtle perceptions of minimal physical cues indicating the opponent's intent, but it appears to happen on its own. The body detects and responds naturally and automatically. Once the intent of the attack is assessed, the action can be intercepted by initiating an attack in defense, as a counterattack to the attack, or simply in response to the intent to attack. Intercepting allows an attack to be redirected away from the intended point of impact. Contact in weapons training is not just weapon on weapon, or wood on wood; contact implies a connection, *musubi,* that allows intuitive as well as actual communication.

Contact can be initiated mentally and physically. Some will talk about the initial eye contact. Eye contact—the eyes being the window to the heart, mind, and soul of an individual—sets the stage and foretells the outcome for the rest of the encounter. Others suggest that contact can be made by means of an energy or kinesthetic sense, by just feeling the attacker's presence and intent. Contact may be auditory, by hearing the attacker's approach. Without contact, there is no attack or defense, and there is no aikido. O'Sensei Morihei Ueshiba would instruct students not to focus their eyes on the weapon, for one can then easily be deceived. Rather look through your opponent's eyes, using your peripheral vision and all the other senses to simply perceive and be aware, rather than focus. This is extremely important due to the extended range and potential danger of weapons training in aikido.

Once contact is established, it should be maintained in one fluid movement, throughout the execution of the technique, and even during the resolution of the encounter or attack. Initially, techniques are practiced in a step-by-step, systematic manner or pattern. This allows the practitioner to focus on the correct form at different stages of the technique's execution. Eventually, the follow-through of one stage, or phase, naturally and fluidly follows the momentum and inertia into the next. This ongoing flowing execution is characteristic of aikido. The weapon of aikido never stops. Defense flows into offense that flows into defense. Never stopping, all weapons training techniques enter and blend into one motion.

The contours of the body, or weapon, provide a ready-made natural path from the extremity to the center of the body. Follow the contour. Following the contour allows one to stay in contact and maintain sensitivity throughout the execution of the technique. It also prevents one from working against the structural strengths of the body, and allows fluid, direct application of the concepts of aikido. As an attacker extends his arm and weapon, he provides a pathway by sliding his weapon along the contour to hit the target as a strike, *atemi,* or to provide leverage for a throw, *nage,* or for take-down and control.

The position that generates the most power is one that allows power to flow from behind and beneath. With the hands and weapon in front of the body, the hips or center moves forward from behind to generate and extend full body power. When stepping and turning *tenkan,* in a circular step, pull the rear hip back to generate more power than twisting or turning from the front. Rather than pushing a weapon down from above, allowing the weight to rest on the underside of the weapon utilizes the force and natural law of gravity to add power to the striking motion.

One of the unique characteristics of aikido movement and technique is the use of circular motion instead of a linear path. Following the natural laws of circular motion and force facilitates the availability and use of both centrifugal and centripetal force. Centrifugal force moves away from the center, and centripetal force moves toward the center. The circular path of aikido techniques pulls into the center using centripetal force, while those appendages on the circumference of the circle tend to move away from the center. While the center hub of the circle moves slowly, the outer rim or circumference moves faster. Pulling the butt end of the weapon into the center facilitates a faster and more powerful motion on the end of the weapon when it follows a circular path.

Along with circular motion is the range of motion as the circle of power. Every weapon has a specific range of motion and power. The closer to the center of that circular range of motion, the less power there is. Likewise, an attack loses power beyond the circumference of the circular path of power, or beyond the attacking limb's range of motion.

Movement in aikido makes full use of the natural laws of momentum and inertia. Momentum is the property of a moving body or weapon, a constant force exerted by virtue of its mass weight and velocity, until it comes to rest. The momentum of the weapon allows it to continue its path along the line of attack with optimal force toward a specific point of intended impact and damage. The law of inertia states that something in motion tends to stay in motion, and something at rest tends to stay at rest. This accounts for the dynamic—versus static or stationary—ease with which aikido practitioners move, throw, and even pin larger, more powerful, opponents.

Do only that which adds to, and is necessary for, successful execution of an aikido technique. Minimize any motion. Relaxation minimizes tension and maximizes fluidity of motion and responsiveness. In throwing an individual, it is often enough to break his balance and allow him to fall. In the application of a joint lock, just enough pressure to gain compliance and submission is enough, without the necessity of inflicting pain or doing damage. It is natural initially to feel tense while training with aikido weapons. Eventually, with honest and genuine training, one remains relaxed while being attacked by or attacking with the wooden weapons of aikido.

The technical execution, application, and utilization of leverage and pivot points greatly enhance the power of aikido. Leverage generates more power by using a fulcrum type of pressure to move an object with less effort than if force were applied directly to the object. A slight movement at one end of a weapon can produce a large impact at the other end.

The technical execution and application of the wave motion is to move up-down-up, down-up-down, in-out-in, out-in-out, forward-back-forward, or back-forward-back. The movement takes into account the resistance offered to an initial move, accepts it until the resistance is released, and then immediately reapplies the directional intention to the now emptied and open pathway.

Sequential Execution

There are four sequential stages of aikido technique execution: (1) enter and blend, (2) redirect and unbalance, (3) throw or control, and (4) let go and move away.

The first stage, enter and blend, applies to the utilization of weapons. Entering means to move toward, and in synchronization with, another. Blending means to become one and move as a unit rather than as two individuals. When attacked by a weapon, rather than retreat, an aikido practitioner allows the attack to continue on its attack line without resistance, while stepping off the attack line and entering or bridging the distance to the attacker.

The second stage is to redirect the attack and unbalance the attacker. Blending with an attack often includes just not being at the point of intended impact. Extending past the point of intended impact reduces the power and control exerted by the strike. As one blends with the strike, one begins to take control and redirect it. Usually following a circular path, this redirection continues towards a kuzushi, or until the momentum and inertia create unbalance. An unbalanced opponent or attacker is easiest to handle. He will follow the redirection in an attempt to regain balance. The principle of redirect and unbalance applies to facing any opponent, with or without a weapon.

The third stage is to throw or control the attacker. While many people do not immediately think of weapons as instruments for throwing an attacker or applying a control technique, they actually work very well. Perhaps the unexpectedness of their utilization in this fashion adds to their effectiveness. While there may be some debate about atemi, or striking, in aikido, there is no debate about the effectiveness and efficiency of utilizing a weapon specifically designed for that purpose. Atemi in empty-hand aikido techniques is often reserved for distraction and unbalancing, unless it is more of a self-defense situation and application. In weapons training, striking, throwing, and control are all viable and valuable options.

After successfully completing the execution of an aikido technique, one must learn to let go and move on. A slight pause before letting go allows for a sense of closure and completion. *Zanshin* is the term for the idea of a lingering spirit or connection. Once the encounter is completed, however, let go and move on the next attacker or opponent. This is especially true in *randori* practice against sequential multiple attackers, or in a real self-defense situation where one can never assume there is only one attacker.

Conceptual Execution

Shoshin and *mushin* are two very important frames of minds to continually cultivate and maintain. Shoshin is "beginner's mind," and mushin is a calm and empty mind. Shoshin is the openness and awe of the beginner's mind. It is the mind ready and available to learn. Mushin is the serene, unoccupied mind that, through years of disciplined training, is able to allow the body to be aware and respond with spontaneous execution of the appropriate technique.

Shizan-tai is a relaxed, natural state of being. The concept of natural movement and natural forces is very common in aikido. Maintaining a relaxed state, both physically and mentally, allows one to respond appropriately with greater effectiveness and efficiency. A state of being is different from a state of doing in that being relaxed and natural, without fear, may be all the doing that is necessary.

Metsuke is the soft eye focus that facilitates better utilization of the peripheral vision to be aware of motion and to help maintain a sense of physical, emotional, and mental calm. Metsuke perceives as if looking into the distance, without focusing or stopping the eyes or mind on any one thing. Without attachment to any one thing, all things are seen and perceived for what they are. "Seeing without looking = perceiving" (Random 1977, p. 78). Looking implies looking for something specific, while perceiving means to be aware of what is there. Metsuke also facilitates the ability to perceive and distinguish shapes, contours, and textures that do not fit a specific context, giving advance notice and the ability to respond proactively and protectively. Too often, in weapons work, the eyes focus on the weapon. This is a mistake, since it leaves the vision and reaction fixated on only one aspect of the opponent or attacker.

Ma-ai is the concept of cultivation and maintenance of proper combative distance. Too far away, and the technique is ineffective because one is outside the circle of power. Too close, and the technique is ineffective as well. The beginning ready ma-ai is often the distance required to have the tips of the weapons touching, so that one step can deliver the single lethal strike.

Musubi, or connection, is required for the successful, effective, and efficient execution of any aikido technique. Musubi, establishing a connection, is as much psychological as physical. In order to respond in rhythm and synchronization with an opponent or attacker, contact and mental connection must exist. The attacker or opponent is no longer seen, experienced, thought of, or responded to as a separate entity. When either body moves, they both move as one unit. When you move, the opponent or attacker moves, and vice versa. The two separate individuals now become one. This is a philosophical, as well as physical and psychological, element of aikido that makes it a harmonious and spiritual practice. Once the two of you are connected, what happens to your opponent or attacker now happens to you.

Irimi means to enter into. Rather than disconnect and move away, irimi means to connect by moving into. Moving away sets up a chase mentality in the attacker and leaves the defender still vulnerable and available for further pursuit and attack. In irimi, you move toward the attacker, off the line of attack, intercepting the attack and taking the initiative. This interruption and interception often takes the attacker by surprise; finding you closer, not farther away, unbalances the attacker both mentally and physically.

Awase means to blend. Many say that the essence of aikido is the blending with an attack to the point that the blending itself unbalances the attacker. Blending comprises all the concepts of aikido. To successfully blend with an attack, one must connect with the rhythmic movement and timing so they bond and become one motion. The blending movement will naturally be followed by the attacker because of the perfect timing that permits physical or energetic contact and connection while leading or redirecting the attack. This blending, awase, is mental, physical, and ki.

Kuzushi means balance. What makes aikido effective and efficient is the ability to unbalance an attacker or opponent, from the moment that contact and connection, mental and physical, are made. It is hard for an attacker to pursue, or continue to attack, while he is concerned with the higher priority of maintaining his own balance. Many nage-waza (throwing techniques), especially the *kokyu-nage* (breath or timing throws), unbalance an attacker simply by emptying the space he needs for support, by moving out of range and throwing off his kuzushi. Some of the weapons techniques shown later in this book will demonstrate the use of the weapon and avoiding the attacker as a means of neutralizing the attack and unbalancing the opponent.

Zanshin means a lingering mind and spirit connection that exists and continues long after the successful execution and completion of the technique. With the exception of randori (against multiple attackers), a slight pause at the end of the technical execution establishes a mental connect that lasts and leaves a lingering impression. The last chapter of this book is called "Zanshin," because after your reading is completed, the information presented here will have a lasting effect on your wooden weapons training, and hopefully will establish a lingering connection with the authors.

Ki

"*Ki* refers to a universal life force or energy which connects us all physically and spiritually" (Dang and Seiser 2003, p. 112). Ki is both internal and universally external.

Without ki, there is no aikido. Ki is the essence of life. Ki is energy. Ki affects the union of body and mind. Ki is controlled and directed by the mind. Conscious discipline and training develops and extends ki into every momentum and every movement. The best way to develop ki is through consistent and persistent practice. It is important to maintain proper structural alignment. The body is like a hose that one is trying to run water through. If there is a kink in the hose, then the water cannot run smoothly and fluidly. Structural alignment and proper posture are like taking the kinks out of the hose and allowing the water to flow freely. Therefore, before an emphasis is put on developing and extending ki, it is important to gain some level of proficiency in technical execution while maintaining proper alignment and posture.

After avoiding all attacks by a wooden sword, O'Sensei Morihei Ueshiba stood before a persimmon tree and realized the true spirit of budo was the loving protection of all beings.

An old expression states that if you can see it, you can be it. Visualize the ki flow. Visualize the energy from your center, in the hip region, extending out beyond your hands, beyond the technique. Visualize the energy, like that water through the hose, flowing out in the direction you are pointing. This visualization informs and directs the ki flow. The mind can develop and direct ki. Mental calmness and training are very important in ki development, which influences all aspects of aikido training.

Sensei Tohei, founder of *ki-aikido* and one of the original top instructors, is credited with bringing aikido to the world outside Japan. He developed four rules for the development of ki (Tohei 1973, p. 2; 1976, p. 15; 1978, p. 27). They are to relax completely, let the weight settle to the underside, focus on the one point, and extend ki.

To develop, generate, and utilize ki, the body must be completely relaxed. This is not the state of relaxation that would cause the body to fall over, but rather the relaxation that allows the body to move freely and lets internal and universal energy run freely through it. Tension in the body prevents the free flow of blood and neural impulse signals. With relaxation, breathing becomes deeper, increasing oxygenation and energy. Relax deeply and completely while maintaining proper alignment and posture.

It is natural for the weight of an object to settle or rest on the underside. In exercises such as the unbendable arm test, a test of ki extension and mental focus, instead of imagining holding the arm from above, feel it supported from below. Visualize and feel the body supported from the underside. While holding a wooden weapon, sense that the alignment and support from the underside of your arm extends to and through the weapon to the tip of the weapon. When striking, feel the weapon being pulled down from beneath naturally rather than being pushed down from above.

Allow the focus and movement to be on and originate from the "one point." As explained above, this one point, or center, is in the hip region. It is the exact center between top and bottom, left and right, front and back. All movement in aikido, including weapons work, originates and aligns with the center. Ki passes through the center point of the body, or *hara*. Physical and mental balance and unity are centered and coordinated from the hara. *Kime* is the gathering of the body's physical and psychical energy into one spot.

Once ki is kime in the hara, it can be extended. Rather than consciously focusing on the physical feelings while executing an aikido technique, focus on the feeling of the energy or ki flow. Eventually, one develops a sense for feeling not only one's own ki flow, but also that of the opponent. Ki extends and penetrates through the opponent's center toward a kuzushi. Breathe in as ki is gathered, and breathe out as ki is extended. Breathe in as you enter and blend with the opponent's momentum and inertia. Breathe out as you execute a throw or apply pressure to an immobilization lock. Breathe in as the weapon is readied, breathe out as the weapon is used to throw, control, or strike.

Kokyu

Closely aligned with ki is the concept of *kokyu*. Kokyu means breath. Kokyu implies the use of ki. The oxygen in the air we breathe is used by the body to physically convert nutrients into energy. Kokyu is the blending of opposites, inhalation and exhalation, that facilitates life.

Kokyu is also about the timing of those opposites. A kokyu-nage technique is executed by entering, blending, and aligning with the opponent's momentum and inertia, his ki, with such precise timing that it is as if the breath alone throws him.

Training

The principles of training in empty-hand aikido apply equally to weapons training. The four levels of training include unconscious incompetence, conscious incompetence, conscious competence, and unconscious competence. The goal is to evolve from unconscious incompetence (it doesn't work, but you don't know it) to unconscious competence (it works all by itself). Mastery is the passage through the conscious stages of training. The fastest way through the conscious incompetence and competence stages is to slow down and stay conscious of the repetitive practice necessary to habituate the neural, muscular, skeletal, behavioral, mental, and psychological pathways and patterns. The training plateaus are the most important stages for working on conscious competence, for it is then that the body is not necessarily learning anything new but polishing what it already knows and habituating that knowledge into muscle or neural pathways, thus facilitating unconscious memory and competence.

There are many levels or types of training.

Keiko means training or practice. Keiko is the basics, the fundamentals. Keiko is the normal practice session or workout. Basic to keiko is *kata*. *Kata* usually is a specific prearranged solo form or pattern; in aikido, however, kata is a specific prearranged pattern of exchange of technique. In other words, kata is having the opponent approach and attack in a specific and predetermined way, allowing you to practice a specific and predetermined technique. Kata has always been used to preserve the technique of a style. Kata allows repetitive, realistic training in techniques that would be too dangerous or lethal to train with a partner. Kata can also be used in solo training without a partner by practicing the prearranged kata patterns in the air while imagining an attacker or opponent, allowing full momentum, force, and follow-through. Kata follows a step-by-step sequence that is to be followed each and every time. Eventually the sequence loses its steps and becomes one fluid, yet often slow, motion. In the initial keiko training level, one learns the basic techniques and patterns and stays within the form, perfecting it before practicing variations or freeform execution.

Shugyo means rigorous daily training. This is one level up from keiko. The training is harder and, because of the frequency, it becomes more of a way of life than an activity one simply does. Because of the vigorousness of the training, one is less able to stay conscious of everything, and the technique and training become more automatic and trusted. The pace of training increases. The execution of the techniques becomes smoother and faster, a single unit rather than the acceleration-slowdown pattern of the keiko training. Shugyo is a time for refining and experimenting with variations outside the form of the technique.

The *misogi* level involves esoteric and often severe purification rituals, which are a part of aikido wooden weapons training. Misogi is the training that aims at overcoming both oneself, as an individual learned ego identity, and the form of the technique. The goal of misogi is *sumikiri,* a total clarity of body and mind, and *satori* (enlightenment). One of the most commonly recognized actual practices of misogi is standing in a meditative state under a cold waterfall. Keiko as everyday training can become shugyo and misogi if undertaken with the correct intent and intensity.

Ultimately, training should be done with the goal of *gakemusu-aiki,* the spontaneous execution of the appropriate technique, at the appropriate time, against the appropriate attack, as if guided and directed by *kami,* or spirit. At this level, training becomes a way of life, or *tashinamu,* training for its own sake without recognition or promotion.

The serious student of aikido will progressively and naturally undertake weapons training with the wooden sword, staff, and knife as an integral component of practice. Extending the technical, sequential, and conceptual application of empty-hand aikido techniques into weapons training will build proficiency and confidence. As in all aikido training, the student should receive competent instruction and train with honest and genuine intent and intensity. Relax, breathe, and enjoy the training.

Chapter 2

BOKEN: WOODEN SWORD

The use of bladed weapons is very old. The earliest Japanese swords were made of stone or wood. It was not until the second century B.C. that metal was forged into the sword shape resembling the continental Asian prototypes. Eventually, the sword evolved into the single-edged, curved-bladed, two-handed design commonly perceived as distinctively Japanese.

2-1: Bowing with the boken

The sword has always been the central weapon in the martial hierarchy. It was the symbol of the ruling warrior class. Sword design and tactics were a priority for military leaders. Skill in forging a razor-sharp edge, along with swordsmanship, brought fear and respect to the bushi or samurai. The sword became his profession, his tradition, his honor, and his soul.

As one begins to study the way of the sword, images of great samurai emerge. Perhaps the most famous swordsman of Japan was Miyamoto Musashi (1584–1645). He learned swordsmanship from his father, a reputable swordsman, and at thirteen years of age he fought and killed Master Arima of the *Shinto-ryu.* He fought and won sixty-six fights in his lifetime. In his final duel against Sasaki, Musashi used a wooden sword. At age sixty, he retired and lived a life of poverty, seclusion, and reflection. His instruction on sword tactics, *The Book of Five Rings,* intended for his successor and other trained sword students, has been translated and applied to all types of situations and professions.

Sword Arts

Ken-jutsu and iai-jutsu are the roots of organized sword practice and training. Since they are jutsu systems, they are oriented toward practical combat applications, to incapacitate or kill an enemy. Physical prowess, technical skills, and expert manipulation of the blade are important.

Ken-jutsu is an aggressive style of swordsmanship. Standing squarely before an opponent and raising the bare blade with both hands required great mental calmness, patience, and confidence. The *boken* became popular for training since it was inexpensive, durable, expendable, and practical for competitive nonlethal practice or contests. Kata, or prearranged patterns, were used in this training.

Iai is the art of drawing the sword. Iai-jutsu was developed as a means of getting the sword out of its scabbard quickly, and it is known for its defensive sword drawing. The defensive draw from a passive position and the offensive cut became one swift, lethal motion. Iai-jutsu also used kata for self-training. It is said that when the sword is in the scabbard it is iai; once drawn, it is ken. Returned to its scabbard, the sword is again iai. The iai student practices kata alone from various sitting, crouching, and standing positions. Every angle of attack is studied in detail. Emphasis is placed on physical control, smooth movement, and mental and spiritual balance. The movements of iai include *nukisuke* (drawing), *kiritsuke* (cutting), *chiburui* (clearing the blood), and *noto* (sheathing the blade) (Williams 1975, p. 36). The actual art of cutting or testing the sword is called *tameshi-giri*. Rolled wet straw, *tatami* mats, or bamboo stakes are used as the target to cut through.

Kendo and iai-do developed from ken-jutsu and iai-jutsu as a way to use sword practice for personal development, rather than for combat. In these arts, the blade comes to symbolize a means to an end, with the goal of mental calmness and balance, character building, and spiritual awakening or enlightenment. In this sense, the ken cuts through the inner enemy more than the outer enemies.

Eventually kendo evolved into a sport that uses a *shinai,* or flexible split wooden sword, in order to safeguard competitors in training and judging. In kendo competition, only specific targets are allowed, and metsuke (eye contact) and *kiai* (spirit yell) are very important. The body, the sword, and the yell must be unified on every strike. The four mental poisons to overcome through kendo training are fear, doubt, surprise, and confusion. Meditation and silence are used in kendo to create a mind free of thought and tension, so as to show no vulnerability. Iai-do enjoys a close affiliation with kendo. Modern iai-do teaches the art of breathing and serenity of the spirit through drawing, wielding, and sheathing the sword.

Boken Practice

Aikido comes from the study and art of the sword, or ken. This is not readily apparent on superficial observation of most aikido training and practice. It is only through close observation and study that the basic footwork, body movement, and conceptual framework connecting the sword/ken to the empty hand become obvious and applicable. Practicing the sword/ken with honest and genuine intent and intensity will improve all aspects of one's aikido experience.

Boken Etiquette

As in empty-handed practice, before stepping onto the mat or practice area, slightly bow. Humbly acknowledge the intent to train honestly and safely. When traditionally placed on the right, the sword signifies no hostile intent, since it is harder for most people to draw from that side. Placed on the left, the usual positioning for drawing, the sword signifies some hesitancy or hostile intent. Never place the edge and handle near or toward a host. This is considered an insult. For practical purposes and convenience, the wooden weapons used in training are allowed to be on the left-hand side of the student while in *seiza* (kneeling) position.

Grip

Grip the ken with your right hand forward and your left hand to the rear (Figure 2-2). The right first knuckle rests against the sword guard. The left hand rests with the little finger at the base end of the hilt/handle. Allow about 1.5 inches of distance between the hands. Apply the greatest pressure between the last three fingers and the base of the thumb of each hand. Don't grip the hilt/handle with too much strength or tension. Hold loosely, but firmly, to allow fluidity of movement and extension of ki toward and through the tip of the blade. While you hold the ken with your hands, keep your arms relaxed.

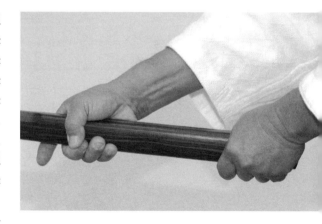

2-2: Gripping the boken

At the point of impact, both hands rotate into the centerline, as if wringing a rag, while pulling slightly back with the front hand and pushing forward with the rear hand. This provides stabilization to the ken.

Stance, Posture, and Position

The typical *kamae*, or posture and stance, centers the body in a relaxed state with the spine aligned and erect. The weapon can be held in a number of positions. In the *jodan* position, the boken is held above the head. The *chudan* position is the middle level with the boken held horizontally. The *gedan* position holds the boken below the horizontal. In the *seidan* position, the boken is aimed or pointed toward the opponent's eyes.

2-3: Ready stance

Ready Stance

To perform the typical ready stance, center and balance your body over your feet, right foot forward (Figure 2-3), with your spine aligned and erect. Hold your rear hand with the end of the sword handle on the centerline, directly in front of your body's center, and right in front of the belt or *hakama* knot. Your forward hand extends the sword directly on the centerline and may point the tip of the sword directly in front, hold the sword horizontally or slightly upward, or point the tip of the sword toward an imaginary or real opponent. Let your arms relax, with the elbows slightly bent. Allow your weight to settle to the underside. Extend ki through the arms and into the sword, controlling the tip. This is the best defensive stance, since it places the sword between the attacker and the intended target. Slight movements allow the sword to be utilized to block or parry. Slight forward movement allows the blade to be used for thrusting or stabbing. The weakness of this position is that performing any full body cuts would require movement away from the intended path, taking more time and leaving some sense of vulnerability.

2-4: Alternative stance

Alternative Stance

An alternative traditional stance positions the sword to the side (Figure 2-4). After assuming a ready stance, step back with your right foot, allowing your right, forward hand to follow backward. Your left hand stabilizes the movement and becomes the pivotal point by not moving off the center. Arms are relaxed with elbows slightly bent. Let your weight settle to the underside. Extend ki through your arms and into the sword. While deceptively appearing more vulnerable, due to the open front, this stance holds the sword in a position ready to strike upward, downward, or to the side, without the need for a preparatory chambering of the weapon. Chambering a strike, empty hand or with weapon, means to pull back or cock the movement before executing a forward thrust or strike. It is already held relaxed in the chambered position, waiting to respond. Some schools or styles prefer to hold the blade closer to the rear leg, as if to hide its existence or importance.

Another traditional stance and sword position, not shown, holds the sword directly overhead, ready for a downward strike.

Attacks or Cuts

There are three major attacks or cuts with the ken. The first is an overhead downward strike called a shomen-uchi, the second is a diagonal oblique strike to the neck called a *yokomen-uchi,* and the third is a straightforward thrust with the tip called a *tsuki.*

2-5: Shomen-Uchi   2-6   2-7: Yokomen-Uchi

Shomen-Uchi: Overhead Downward Strike
From a traditional ready stance and position with the ken forward, raise the sword up and over your head on a vertical circular path following the centerline of the body (Figure 2-5). The raising or lifting movement is executed by rotating at the shoulders, holding your arms and sword in the same position. Hold your elbows slightly bent with your arms relaxed, weight on the underside of your arms, and extend ki through the sword, controlling the tip. Let your body rock back slightly, placing more weight on your rear foot. Inhale. Simultaneously step forward and allow the sword to follow the downward vertical circular path, as you exhale and bring the rear foot slightly forward. The sword should stop abruptly, horizontally in front of the center. Allow your full weight to drop into the strike (Figure 2-6).

To execute a shomen-uchi for the alternative side-holding stance and position, simply raise your hands upward, allowing the sword to follow a vertical circular path up your back and over your head, following the centerline until it reaches the horizontal plane in front of the center of your body.

Yokomen-Uchi: Overhead Diagonal Strike to the Neck
From a traditional ready stance and position with the ken forward, raise the sword up as previously described for a shomen-uchi. Your arms stay relaxed, with elbows bent, rotating at the shoulders. Let your body rock back slightly, placing more weight onto your rear foot, and inhale. Instead of bringing the sword down vertically, as in the shomen-uchi, the yokomen-uchi takes a side

diagonal path of approximately 45 degrees, aiming for the side of the head or neck of your opponent. Your body turns at the waist from the rear hip, keeping your hands and path along the centerline. Exhale and let your weight drop forward on the underside of your arms and sword, and extend ki through both arms and sword while controlling the tip (Figure 2-7).

Tsuki: Straight Thrust

From a traditional ready stance and position with the ken forward, rotate the sword until the blade edge is away from your body. Slide your front foot forward by pushing off your rear foot, as you exhale and thrust out your arms, turning at the waist with the rear hip. Exhale and extend ki out your arms and through the sword, controlling the tip. Do not chamber or pull back the sword before thrusting forward (Figure 2-8).

Draw

To perform a traditional draw, hold the ken at your left hip with your left hand, to simulate a sword in its sheath (Figure 2-9). Place your thumb on top with the blade edge facing up. Your body is relaxed, with your spine aligned and erect. Bring your right hand horizontally across your body, with your palm down, and grasp the handle portion of the ken near your left hand. Pull the ken forward following a vertical circular path, while stepping

2-8: Tsuki   2-9   2-10

back slightly, until the ken stops directly in front and extends out from your body's center and on the centerline. Your left hand simultaneously grasps the end of the ken handle and stabilizes it to the center in front of the belt and hakama knot (Figure 2-10). Traditionally, this draw is done defensively to assume a ready stance.

A slight variation allows the ken to be drawn and brought downward offensively in a shomen-uchi fashion, or as a yokomen-uchi, diagonally or horizontally to the side. To strike diagonally or horizontally from the draw, turn the ken in your hand at the hip before drawing it. Step forward, rather than back, into the cutting movement. Exhale and let your body weight drop onto the underside, into the strike, and extend ki through your arms and into the sword, controlling the tip.

Return

To return the ken to the side, stand in a ready stance. Your right hand simply rotates the ken up then downward on a vertical circular path into your left hand, waiting at your left hip. Step forward. Return your right hand to the right side. Bow.

Alternatively, after striking, abruptly shoot your right hand out to the side, with the ken tip pointing down, and pause (Figure 2-11). Traditionally, in the old times of actual battle, this movement was executed

2-11   2-12   2-13   2-14

in order to flick blood off the blade before returning it to its sheath. If blood remained on the blade, it might dry and cause the sword to be temporarily or permanently stuck in the sheath.

Maintaining a solid balanced stance, bring the ken horizontally across your body (Figure 2-12). As your right hand intercepts the center, rotate the blade edge upward. Your right hand meets your left hand at your left hip. Your left hand is held as if holding a sheath, and it somewhat pinches the top of the blade as if holding it with a cloth to continue cleaning it.

Slide the ken down your left hand, which is held stable at your left hip. A slight down and out movement of the hand facilitates a smooth fluid motion (Figure 2-13). As you turn your rear hip away to provide more room, the ken is drawn until the tip is resting between the thumb and first-finger knuckle of the left hand, pointing into the sheath. Slightly pinching the blade edge with your left thumb and first-finger knuckle, as if wiping it again, slide the ken, blade edge up, into your left hand. Step forward as the returning of the ken is completed (Figure 2-14). Bow.

An excellent exercise is to assume a standing position with the ken at your left side. Quickly draw and cut a yokomen-uchi, holding the ken with only your right hand. Add your left hand, and cut downward in a shomen-uchi. Return the ken to your left side.

Eight-Direction Cut

A traditional solo exercise to perform with the ken is the eight-direction cut. There are three variations. The first is simply to perform an overhead downward shomen-uchi strike in all eight directions. The second is to perform the shomen-uchi in all eight directions, but on the first four directions add a tsuki, and on the last four directions add a shomen-uchi. The third variation performs the shomen-uchi in all eight directions, but on the first four, after executing the shomen-uchi, twist the body to the front before executing the tsuki and chambering the ken. The last four shomen-uchi strikes are like the first two patterns.

The directions of the strikes follow a consistent eight-direction pattern. This can be illustrated by degrees in a circle or hands on a clock. The first strike is directly to the front, or 6:00 o'clock. The second strike is 180 degrees to the rear, or 12:00 o'clock. The third strike is 90 degrees to the right, or 3:00 o'clock. The fourth strike is 180 degrees, or 9:00 o'clock. The next four strikes intersect on the diagonal. The fifth strike is 135 degrees, or where the hour hand would be at 2:30. The sixth strike is 180 degrees from that, or where the hour hand would be at 7:30. The seventh strike is 90 degrees from that, or where the hour hand would be at 10:30. The last and eighth strike is 180 degrees from that, or where the hour hand would be at 4:30.

Standard Eight-Direction Cut

Draw the ken into a ready stance (Figure 2-15). Your body is relaxed with your spine aligned and erect. Maintain metsuke and musubi with an imaginary opponent or target.

Using your shoulders as the pivot point, rotate your arms upward, following a vertical circular path directly up the centerline, until your arms are directly overhead (Figure 2-16) and the ken is touching your spine. Pull your front leg back and let your weight settle on the rear foot. Reverse the direction and bring the ken forward, following the same vertical circular path, following the centerline from the rear, over the head, and down the front. Let your weight settle to the underside of the ken, and step forward. Bring your left, rear, hand into the

2-15   2-16   2-17   2-18

2-19   2-20   2-21

center, which becomes the stabilizing pivot point. Snap the ken down to a horizontal position, executing the first shomen-uchi of the series (Figure 2-17).

Raise your arms up, using your shoulders as the pivot point, and follow a vertical circular path upward. Rotate or pivot at your hips 180 degrees to the rear, at 12:00 o'clock beneath the ken (Figure 2-18). Execute the second shomen-uchi (Figure 2-19).

2-22

2-23

2-24

2-25

2-26

2-27

Raise your arms up, using your shoulders as the pivot point, and follow a vertical circular path upward. Rotate or pivot at your hips 90 degrees to the left, at 3:00 o'clock beneath the ken (Figure 2-20). Execute the third shomen-uchi (Figure 2-21).

Raise your arms up, using your shoulders as the pivot point, and follow a vertical circular path upward. Rotate or pivot at your hips 180 degrees to the rear, at 9:00 o'clock beneath the ken (Figure 2-22). Execute the fourth shomen-uchi (Figure 2-23).

Raise your arms up, using your shoulders as the pivot point, and follow a vertical circular path upward. Rotate or pivot at your hips 135

2-28   2-29   2-30

2-31   2-32

degrees to the right beneath the ken (Figure 2-24). Execute the fifth shomen-uchi (Figure 2-25).

Raise your arms up, using your shoulders as the pivot point, and follow a vertical circular path upward. Rotate or pivot at your hips 180 degrees beneath the ken (Figure 2-26). Execute the sixth shomen-uchi (Figure 2-27).

2-33   2-34   2-35

Raise your arms up, using your shoulders as the pivot point, and follow a vertical circular path upward. Rotate or pivot at your hips 180-degrees beneath the ken (Figure 2-28). Execute the seventh shomen-uchi (Figure 2-29).

Raise your arms up, using your shoulders as the pivot point, and follow a vertical circular path upward. Rotate or pivot at your hips 180 degrees beneath the ken (Figure 2-30). Execute the eighth and final shomen-uchi (Figure 2-31).

To return, abruptly shoot your right hand out to the side with the ken tip pointing down, and pause (Figure 2-32). Maintaining a solid balanced stance, bring the ken horizontally across your body (Figure 2-33). As your right hand intercepts the center, rotate the blade, edge upward. Your right hand meets your left hand at your left hip. Your left hand is held as if holding a sheath, somewhat pinching the top of the blade as if holding it with a cloth to continue cleaning it. Slide the ken down your left hand, which is held stable at your left hip. A slight down and out movement of the hand facilitates a smooth, fluid motion (Figure 2-34). While turning your rear hip away to provide more room, the ken is drawn until the tip is resting between your thumb and the first-finger knuckle of your left hand, and it is then pointed into the sheath. Slightly pinch the blade edge with your left thumb and first-finger knuckle, as if wiping it again, and slide the ken, blade edge up, into your left hand. Step forward as the returning of the ken is completed (Figure 2-35). Bow.

   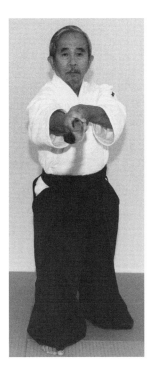

2-36   2-37   2-38   2-39

Eight-Direction Cut: Variation 1

Draw the ken into a ready stance (Figure 2-36). Your body is relaxed with your spine aligned and erect. Maintain metsuke and musubi with an imaginary opponent or target.

Raise your arms up, using your shoulders as the pivot point, and follow a vertical circular path upward (Figure 2-37). Execute the first shomen-uchi (Figure 2-38) and tsuki (Figure 2-39).

Raise your arms up, using your shoulders as the pivot point, and follow a vertical circular path upward. Rotate or pivot at your hips 180 degrees to the rear, at 12:00 o'clock beneath the ken. Execute the second shomen-uchi and tsuki.

Raise your arms up, using your shoulders as the pivot point, and follow a vertical circular path upward. Rotate or pivot at the hips 180 degrees to the right, at 3:00 o'clock beneath the ken. Execute the third shomen-uchi and tsuki.

Raise your arms up, using your shoulders as the pivot point, and follow a vertical circular path upward. Rotate or pivot at the hips 180 degrees to the rear beneath the ken. Execute the fourth shomen-uchi and tsuki.

Raise your arms up, using your shoulders as the pivot point, and follow a vertical circular path upward. Rotate or pivot at your hips 180 degrees beneath the ken. Execute the fifth shomen-uchi.

Raise your arms up, using your shoulders as the pivot point, and follow a vertical circular path upward. Rotate or pivot at your hips 180 degrees beneath the ken. Execute the sixth shomen-uchi.

Raise your arms up, using your shoulders as the pivot point, and follow a vertical circular path upward. Rotate or pivot at your hips 180 degrees beneath the ken. Execute the seventh shomen-uchi.

Raise your arms up, using your shoulders as the pivot point, and follow a vertical circular path upward. Rotate or pivot at your hips 180 degrees beneath the ken. Execute the eighth and final shomen-uchi.

To return, abruptly shoot your right hand out to the side with the ken, tip pointing down, and pause (Figure 2-32). Maintaining a solid balanced stance, bring the ken horizontally across your body (Figure 2-33). As your right hand intercepts the center, rotate the blade, edge upward. Your right hand meets your left hand at your left hip. Your left hand is held as if holding a sheath, somewhat pinching the top of the blade as if holding it with a cloth to continue cleaning it. Slide the ken down your left hand, which is held stable at your left hip. A slight down and out movement of your hand facilitates a smooth, fluid motion (Figure 2-34). While turning your rear hip away to provide more room, the ken is drawn until the tip is resting between your thumb and the first-finger knuckle of your left hand, and is then pointed into the sheath. Slightly pinching the blade edge with your left thumb and first-finger knuckle, as if wiping it again, slide the ken, blade edge up, into your left hand. Step forward (Figure 2-14) as the returning of the ken is completed. Bow.

Eight-Direction Cut: Variation 2

Draw the ken into a ready stance (Figure 2-40). Your body is relaxed, with your spine aligned and erect. Maintain metsuke and musubi with an imaginary opponent or target.

Raise your arms up, using your shoulders as the pivot point, and follow a vertical circular path upward. Execute your first shomen-uchi (Figures 2-41 and 2-42), chamber *omote* (front) (Figure 2-43), and execute a tsuki (Figure 2-44).

Raise your arms up, using your shoulders as the pivot point, and follow a vertical circular path upward. Rotate or pivot at your hips 180 degrees to the rear beneath the ken. Execute the second shomen-uchi, chamber omote, and execute a tsuki.

Raise your arms up, using your shoulders as the pivot point, and follow a vertical circular path upward. Rotate or pivot at your hips 180 degrees to the right beneath the ken. Execute the third shomen-uchi, chamber omote, and execute a tsuki.

Raise your arms up, using your shoulders as the pivot point, and follow a vertical circular path upward. Rotate or pivot at your hips 180 degrees to the rear beneath the ken. Execute the fourth shomen-uchi, chamber omote, and execute a tsuki.

2-40 2-41 2-42 2-43 2-44

Raise your arms up, using your shoulders as the pivot point, and follow a vertical circular path upward. Rotate or pivot at your hips 180 degrees beneath the ken (Figure 2-24). Execute the fifth shomen-uchi (Figure 2-25).

Raise your arms up, using your shoulders as the pivot point, and follow a vertical circular path upward. Rotate or pivot at your hips 180 degrees beneath the ken (Figure 2-26). Execute the sixth shomen-uchi (Figure 2-27).

Raise your arms up, using your shoulders as the pivot point, and follow a vertical circular path upward. Rotate or pivot at your hips 180 degrees beneath the ken (Figure 2-28). Execute the seventh shomen-uchi (Figure 2-29).

Raise your arms up, using your shoulders as the pivot point, and follow a vertical circular path upward. Rotate or pivot at your hips 180 degrees beneath the ken (Figure 2-30). Execute the eighth and final shomen-uchi (Figure 2-31).

To return, abruptly shoot your right hand out to the side, with the ken tip pointing down, and pause (Figure 2-32). Maintaining a solid balanced stance, bring the ken horizontally across the body (Figure 2-33). As your right hand intercepts the center, rotate the blade, edge upward. Your right hand meets your left hand at your left hip. Your left hand is held as if holding a sheath, somewhat pinching the top of the blade as if holding it with a cloth to continue cleaning it. Slide the ken down your left hand, which is held stable at your left hip. A slight down and out movement of the hand facilitates a smooth, fluid motion (Figure 2-34). While turning your rear hip away to provide more room, the ken is drawn until the tip is resting between your thumb and the first-finger knuckle of your left hand, and is then pointed into the sheath. Slightly pinching the blade edge with your left thumb and first-finger knuckle, as if wiping it again, slide the ken, blade edge up, into your left hand. Step forward (Figure 2-14) as the returning of the ken is completed. Bow.

Solo Training Drills
Solo training develops sword-handling technique better than any other practice. Solo training is a time to go slowly, initially, and pay close attention to detail. Without these details, the techniques do not work efficiently or effectively.

A good training exercise is to execute either a shomen-uchi or yokomen-uchi repetitively from a standing position or while walking forward. The strike can come from raising the ken directly overhead or by swinging or rotating the ken close to the side as a blocking motion, alternating sides.

Another great solo training drill is to stand in a ready position with the ken on your left hip. Simultaneously step forward with the right foot while reaching across and drawing the sword into a strike, at about eye level. Step forward again and execute a downward shomen-uchi strike. Stepping back, return the sword/ken to the left hip.

Any sword/ken technique can be used for solo training practice. These techniques can be practiced one at a time, in choreographed kata-type forms or in a freestyle, improvised shadow-boxing style.

Paired Techniques
While solo training can develop technique, it is only through paired technique training that a practitioner can develop distance, timing, and accuracy. Distance is the physical space between an individual and the target; it must be bridged to gain accessibility, and maintained to gain effective execution. Timing is the ability to establish the rhythm and synchronization needed for the ken to reach the target while the target is available. Accuracy is the ability to place the tip or end portion of the blade directly onto and into the intended target area. Training with a live partner provides the opportunity to develop skills and ability that not only look good but also are effective and efficient.

Ken against Ken

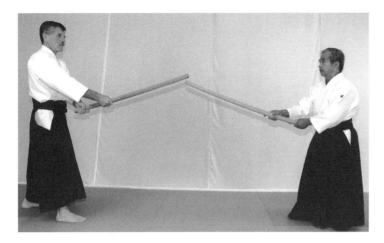

2-45

2-46

2-47

2-48

EXERCISE 1

Assume the appropriate ma-ai and ready stance (Figure 2-45). As the attacker raises his ken to prepare for a shomen-uchi, the defender follows the ken upward, executing his own tsuki to the throat (Figure 2-46). As the defender follows through on the shomen-uchi, the defender steps off the line of attack and slices the ken across the abdomen (Figure 2-47). As the attacker completes the downward strike, the defender pivots and aligns the centers, striking a shomen-uchi to the head or neck (Figure 2-48).

2-49   2-50   2-51

2-52   2-53

EXERCISE 2

Assume the appropriate ma-ai and ready stance. As the attacker raises his ken to prepare for a shomen-uchi, the defender enters, following the ken directly upward and executing a block or cut to the wrist (Figure 2-49). Immediately stepping off the line of
attack and turning or pivoting from the center and hips, the defender executes a side
strike to the ribs (Figure 2-50). Turning the wrist over in a half circle, the defender
strikes the attacker's wrist as he attempts to follow through (Figure 2-51). The defender
follows up with a strike to the neck (Figure 2-52) and again to the wrist (Figure 2-53).

2-54

2-55

2-56

EXERCISE 3

Assume the appropriate ma-ai and ready stance (Figure 2-54). As the attacker raises his ken to prepare for a shomen-uchi downward strike, the defender enters immediately, off the attack line, and strikes to the attacker's abdominal area (Figure 2-55). Turning or pivoting from the center and executing a tenkan (circular step), the defender allows the attacker the forward momentum of his strike while executing a shomen-uchi to the attacker's neck (Figure 2-56).

Ken against Jo

To gain further adaptation and flexibility in training and confidence in execution, it is important to train against a variety of weapons. Each weapon will alter the technique, since the means of attack and defense vary with the weapon, as do the range and angle of attack. Since two of the primary weapons used in aikido training are the ken and jo, it becomes important that one train in both. This way, no matter which weapon you hold in your hand—or even if you have no weapon—your mind and body are trained to calmly face any opponent, with any weapons, at any distance.

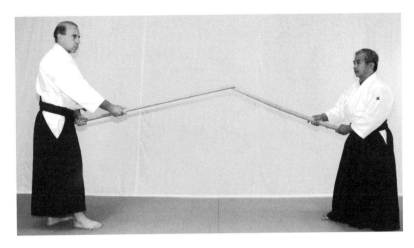

2-57

2-58

2-59

2-60

EXERCISE 1

Assume the appropriate ma-ai and ready stance (Figure 2-57). As the attacker raises his jo, the defender enters immediately, striking the rib area with his ken (Figure 2-58). As the attacker continues the downward momentum of the shomen-uchi strike, the defender blends with the attacker by executing a tenkan to the rear while intercepting, capturing, and controlling the attacker's hand, in order to redirect and unbalance him (Figure 2-59). Pivoting from the center and hip, the defender reverses direction by executing *kote-gaeshi* to the wrist and striking a yokomen-uchi to the attacker's neck (Figure 2-60).

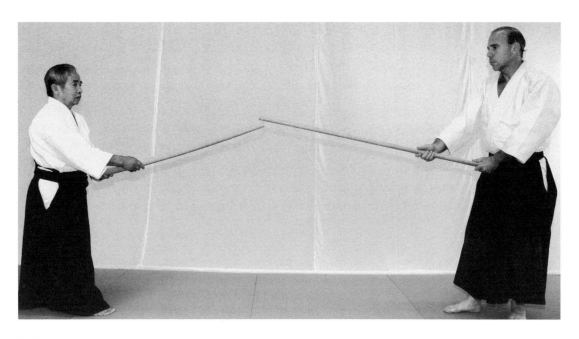

2-61

2-62

2-63

EXERCISE 2

Assume the appropriate ma-ai and ready stance (Figure 2-61). As the attacker raises his jo overhead to prepare the strike, the defender enters immediately, raising his ken to attack the throat, thus intercepting and interrupting the attack (Figure 2-62). As the attacker attempts to follow through on the shomen-uchi, the defender steps forward, off the line of attack, and delivers a horizontal strike with his ken to the rib area (Figure 2-63).

Sword-Taking: Empty Hand against Ken

One of the cornerstones of aikido training is achieving adaptability and flexibility so that eventually the techniques will flow in spontaneous response to any attack, without thought. Facing a weapon with another weapon is a step in developing the ability to judge and bridge distances. Facing a weapon with empty hands is yet a further step in training to develop confidence in one's own ability and the effectiveness of aikido techniques. Since aikido comes from a sword art, the ability to face the sword empty-handed maintains that feudal history while conditioning the body and mind to face escalating conflict situations calmly, with open hands.

EXERCISE 1

Assume the appropriate ma-ai and ready stance (Figure 2-64). As the attacker raises his ken in preparation to attack, the defender enters directly and strikes atemi to the face (Figure 2-65). Keeping the hand to the inside, the defender blends with the attack and redirects it, while performing a tenkan to the rear on a horizontal circular path (Figure 2-66). Changing to a vertical circular path, the defender executes kote-gaeshi (Figure 2-67). After completing the throw, the defender maintains control of the weapon (Figure 2-68), turning the attacker over and disarming him (Figure 2-69).

2-64

2-65

2-66

2-67

2-68

2-69

EXERCISE 2

Assume the appropriate ma-ai and ready stance. As the attacker strikes with a shomen-uchi, the defender immediately steps off the line of attack, and enters by executing a tenkan to the front (Figure 2-70), capturing and controlling the weapon by grabbing the handle. The defender follows the attacker's momentum, then unbalances and throws the attacker (Figure 2-71), while taking his ken away (Figure 2-72).

2-70

2-71

2-72

EXERCISE 3

Assume the appropriate ma-ai and ready stance. As the attacker attempts a shomen-uchi attack, the defender immediately enters, intercepts, and interrupts the attack by capturing and controlling both the wrist and elbow of the attacker (Figure 2-73). Stepping with a tenkan, the defender gets behind the attacker and continues the downward momentum of the attack (Figure 2-74) until the attacker is thrown and disarmed (Figure 2-75).

2-73

2-74

2-75

The Bow

After study or practice with the ken, hold it up horizontally and give a slight bow to the *shomen* (see page 29, Figure 2-1). This acknowledges respect and gratitude to O'Sensei Morihei Ueshiba for the art he has given us. The practice of bowing after every training session also reminds one that the art of the ken is a spiritual, as well as a physical, discipline. As you end a training session, remember the physical skills and spiritual qualities you have developed.

Chapter 3

JO: WOODEN STAFF

In sixteenth-century Japan, a time of great feudal fighting, a samurai named Muso Gonnosuke trained in all weapons. He studied at the Katori Shinto-ryu and the Kashima Shinto-ryu. He particularly enjoyed roaming Japan and challenging masters, armed only with a wooden staff called a *bo,* which was a very common means of training at the time. Initially, he never suffered defeat. Eventually his fame spread, and he finally met and fought the great sword master Miyamoto Musashi in 1606 in Akashi, in the Harima province of Japan. Musashi, using only a wooden sword, initially defeated Muso Gonnosuke's bo attack and spared his life. In defeat and despair, Muso Gonnosuke retreated and began to lead a life of meditation and asceticism, while still training with the bo. Gonnosuke had a divine dream. After experiencing insight and interpreting his vision, he reevaluated his favored bo weapon and made a shorter stick, the jo. Its shorter length allowed him to

3-1: Bowing with the jo

get closer to strike vulnerable body points. Gonnosuke developed twelve basic movements and named his art jo-jutsu. Later, using the shorter jo, Muso Gonnosuke defeated Musashi—the great sword master's only defeat—and returned Musashi's favor by sparing his life. The art of the jo became known as *Shinto Muso-ryu,* and was the exclusive property of the Kuroda samurai. There is no evidence that aikido founder O'Sensei Morihei Ueshiba directly studied this style of jo fighting; however, he choose the jo to be one of the few weapons of choice in aikido training.

Bo-Jutsu and Jo-Jutsu

Bo-jutsu and jo-jutsu have never lost their combat effectiveness, because they were initially ideal for defeating but not killing. *Jodo* is a modern attempt to evolve the more combative jutsu system into a sport, or do. The bo is usually any length over five feet, with a diameter over one inch. A jo is anything less than the five-foot length of the bo. The use of the jo was greatly influenced by O'Sensei Morihei Ueshiba's training in bladed weapons, such as the spear and bayonet.

Stance

There are three basic stances or postures in working with the jo: a regular standing stance and two ready stances.

3-2: Standing stance

Standing Stance

The regular standing stance is relaxed with your spine aligned and erect (Figure 3-2). The jo is held in front on the centerline, with your forward hand. Your eyes maintain metsuke.

Ready Stance 1

The first ready stance positions the jo directly in front of the center (Figure 3-3). The jo extends horizontally or slightly upward, targeted toward the opponent's eyes.

Ready Stance 2

The second ready stance positions the jo back at a 45-degree angle, held downward (Figure 3-4). This deceptive position provides an opening, inviting attack, but minimizes the response time, since the jo is already held in a chambered position.

From the typical kamae stance, center your body in a relaxed state, with your spine aligned and erect. As with the boken, the jo can be held in a number of positions. In the jodan position, the jo is held above the head. The chudan position is the middle level, with the jo held horizontally. The gedan position holds the jo below horizontal. The seidan positions the jo to be aimed or pointed toward the opponent's eyes.

3-3: Ready Stance 1   3-4: Ready Stance 2

Grip

Identical to the ken grip, the jo is traditionally held with the right hand forward and the left hand at the center (Figure 3-5). The jo is held firmly with the hands, not arms, applying pressure between the base of the thumb and the last three fingers.

3-5: Gripping the jo

Grab

There are two traditional ways of grabbing the jo to move it from the standing position to the ready position. The jo can be grabbed from the top or the bottom.

Top Grab

From the standing position, with your left hand holding the jo in front on the centerline, your right hand grabs the top of the jo (Figure 3-6). Keeping your left hand in place and using it as a pivot point, bring your right hand downward, settling the jo in a horizontal position (Figure 3-7). Maintaining your left hand as a forward guide, pull the jo back and slightly upward with your right hand (Figure 3-8). While you still maintain your left front hand, your right hand shoots the jo directly forward with a tsuki (Figure 3-9).

3-6   3-7   3-8   3-9

Bottom Grab

From the standing position (Figure 3-10), turn your front left hand until the jo becomes horizontal and meets your rear right hand, which is held at the center (Figure 3-11). Maintaining the position and using your front left hand as a guide, slide the jo backward by pulling with your rear right hand (Figure 3-12). Keeping your front left hand stable as a guide, snap your right hand forward, executing a tsuki (Figure 3-13).

3-10   3-11   3-12   3-13

Slide

Varying the grip position adds torque and power to a weapon by varying its lengths. The jo can strike with both ends. If held at its center, the jo has a limited range. Sliding the hands from one end of the jo to the other gives the jo an increased effective range. The sliding of the hands also provides some addition centripetal and centrifugal force to the torque and power of the jo. Pulling the jo into the center with minimal movement at one end will increase its speed and power at the other end, as it travels the radius to the circumference of the attack path. Since one can often detect and predict a weapon's path by the hands, this sleight-of-hand tactic is also somewhat deceiving.

From a ready position in which the jo is horizontal (Figure 3-14), draw the jo backward with the rear hand (Figure 3-15). Deceptively, rather than thrust the jo forward, your rear hand comes forward, sliding down the jo toward your front hand as your body rotates, adding power and torque to a horizontal strike (Figure 3-16).

3-14

3-15

3-16

Basic Strikes

Besides the tsuki (straight thrust) and the horizontal slide, the other three basic strikes are the shomen-uchi (overhead downward strike), the yokomen-uchi (diagonal strike), and the low sweep.

Shomen-Uchi

From the front ready position (Figure 3-17), inhale while raising the jo by keeping your arms relaxed and rotating from the shoulders directly up the centerline. Follow a vertical circular path until the jo is behind your body and your hands are directly overhead (Figure 3-18). Exhaling, reverse the direction and snap the jo downward, retracing the vertical circular path. Allow your weight to rest on the underside of your arms and the jo. As your back hand comes to the center, bring the snap to a horizontal position with your front right hand (Figure 3-19), to execute a shomen-uchi.

Yokomen-Uchi

From the front ready position (Figure 3-20), inhale and raise the jo by keeping your arms relaxed and rotating from the shoulders directly up the centerline, following a vertical circular path until the jo is behind your

3-17

3-18

3-19

body and your hands are directly overhead (Figure 3-21). This time, rather than deliver a shomen-uchi, exhale and snap the overhead jo forward on a yokomen-uchi diagonal strike (Figure 3-22).

3-20　　　　　　　3-21　　　　　　　　3-22

3-23　　　　　　3-24

Low Sweep

From the ready position with the jo held low and to the rear (Figure 3-23), twist at the center or waist in order to put your hips behind the low sweep (Figure 3-24). The low sweep can be used as a strike to the legs, a block to low strikes, or an actual sweep to the legs.

Solo Training Twirl

Twirling the jo is a great solo training exercise. The twirl helps an individual get the feel of the jo and the flow of movement. While the twirl may appear spectacular in observation and demonstration, it has limited practical application other than possible visual intimidation. The twirl should be practiced on a regular basis. It can help loosen up the body and provide yet another opportunity to practice the physical alignment and conceptual application of aikido.

From a ready stance (Figure 3-25), with the jo in front of your body, begin a vertical circular path to the rear by turning from the center or hips (Figure 3-26). Continue the vertical twirl in front of your body by turning the center or hips (Figure 3-27) until the continuation of the twirl arrives at the opposite side rear (Figure 3-28). Step forward and execute a shomen-uchi (Figure 3-29).

An alternative solo exercise is to place both hands in the middle of the jo and twirl a figure eight from one side to the other in a continuous motion. Practice both the downward and upward figure eight.

Thirty-One-Count Jo Kata

It is said that O'Sensei Ueshiba created the thirty-one-count jo kata in order to preserve the heritage of his favorite jo techniques and their aikido application. A kata is a prearranged or choreographed series or sequence of techniques. The kata is used to ensure some authenticity in the transmission of the art of aikido. The thirty-one-count jo kata is an excellent means of solo practice and training as well as a direct connection to a very rich heritage.

3-25

3-26

3-27

3-28

3-29

3-30   3-31   3-32   3-33

1. Rei (bow). Assume a ready stance (Figure 3-30). Step off the line of attack. Execute a tsuki (Figure 3-31).
2. Step back on the line. Lift your rear hand for a block (Figure 3-32).
3. Step back off line. Execute a tsuki (Figure 3-33).
4. Step back on line. Raise the jo and block with both hands toward the center (Figure 3-34).
5. Step forward. Execute a shomen-uchi (Figure 3-35).
6. Step forward again. Execute a shomen-uchi (Figure 3-36).
7. Turn at the center or hips, raise your hands, rotate 180 degrees (Figure 3-37). Execute a shomen-uchi (Figure 3-38).
8. Step forward. Execute a shomen-uchi (Figure 3-39).
9. Turn your body 180 degrees to the front, then sweep the jo from high to low rear (Figure 3-40).

3-34

3-35

3-36

3-37

3-38

3-39

3-40

3-41   3-42   3-43   3-44

10. Step forward. Execute a high block or strike (Figure 3-41).

11. Step forward. Execute a shomen-uchi (Figure 3-42).

12. Rotate jo with your forward hand, catching the jo at the center. Pull downward (Figure 3-43).

13. Execute a tsuki (Figure 3-44).

14. Execute a high block (Figure 3-45).

15. Step forward. Execute a shomen-uchi (Figure 3-46).

16. Pull back. Slide the jo backward through your hand to a low rear strike (Figure 3-47) or rear ready position.

17. Step back. Turn from the center. Execute a low sweep (Figure 3-48).

18. Switch hands (Figure 3-49).

19. Execute a low tsuki (Figure 3-50).

20. Step forward. Kneel. Execute a shomen-uchi (Figure 3-51).

3-45

3-46

3-47

3-48

3-49

3-50

3-51

3-52   3-53   3-54   3-55

21. Slide the jo through both hands to a rear strike or ready position (Figure 3-52).
22. Step forward. Raise the jo, and execute a jab (Figure 3-53).
23. Rotate the jo in your forward hand. Execute a downward tap to horizontal position (Figure 3-54).
24. Execute a tsuki (Figure 3-55).
25. Execute a tsuki (Figure 3-56).
26. Slide the jo through your hands to a back low strike or rear ready position (Figure 3-57).
27. Step forward. Execute a low sweep (Figure 3-58).
28. Jab (Figure 3-59).
29. Rotate the jo in your front hand (Figure 3-60).
30. Execute a tsuki (Figure 3-61).
31. Switch feet. Execute a shomen-uchi (Figure 3-62). Ready stance. Rei.

3-56

3-57

3-58

3-59

3-60

3-61

3-62

Complementary Paired Kata

While solo exercise is an excellent way to develop technique, it is only through paired practice that one develops distance skills, timing, and accuracy. There are many possible variations for practicing the thirty-one-step jo kata. What follows is only a suggestion.

1. Rei. Ready stance. With your left foot forward, step in and thrust with a tsuki.
2. Parry the stick over and execute a tsuki.
3. Stand still, hold a ready position.
4. Tsuki.
5. Step back, tenkan, perform a high block parry, execute a yokomen-uchi.
6. Move one step forward, execute a reverse strike or shomen-uchi.
7. Stand still in a ready position.
8. Step forward.
9. Step back, raise the jo overhead, while avoiding low sweep.
10. Step forward and begin a shomen-uchi, receiving a hit at your wrist with your hand raised.
11. Finish the shomen-uchi.
12. Pull back to a ready position.
13. Tsuki.
14. Step back, tenkan, execute a yokomen-uchi or high block/parry.
15. Step forward, execute a shomen-uchi.
16. Hold.
17. Step back, low sweep/parry.
18. Tsuki.
19. Step back, pick up rear of the jo, low parry.
20. Low parry/block or yokomen-uchi.
21. Hold.
22. Begin a shomen-uchi, but when the jo is raised, it is intercepted with a reverse strike or jab to the stomach.
23. Avoid the hit by stepping back, then strike forward/jab.
24. Rotate the jo (change hands), low downward parry/block.
25. Rotate the jo (change hands). Parry down on top of the jo.
26. Tsuki.
27. Step back, low sweep/parry.
28. Step back, high parry with a reverse grip, or sweep horizontally with your hands near center of the jo.
29. Step back, raise the jo above your head, starting a shomen-uchi.
30. Finish the shomen-uchi.
31. Tsuki. Ready stance. Rei.

Paired Techniques

As stated earlier, solo practice trains technique, while paired practice develops distance skills, timing, and accuracy. Since aikido uses the energy and momentum of an attack, weapons training also requires the interaction of training against a variety of other weapons, the jo and ken, as well as empty hands.

Jo against Ken

EXERCISE 1

Establish the appropriate ma-ai (Figure 3-63). As the attacker pulls back to execute a shomen-uchi with the ken, the defender enters and blends with the movement, following the arm upward with the jo to the throat (Figure 3-64). As the attacker continues the downward shomen-uchi momentum, the defender steps off the line of attack and delivers a horizontal slide strike to the ribs (Figure 3-65). The defender then threads the jo through the attacker's arms (Figure 3-66). Pivoting tenkan behind the attacker, the defender begins a vertical circular path down with the attacker's hands and up behind his shoulders (Figure 3-67). Continuing the momentum of the throw, and blending with the momentum of the attack, the defender throws the attacker (Figure 3-68).

3-63

3-64

3-65

3-66

3-67

3-68

EXERCISE 2

Establish the appropriate ma-ai and ready position (Figure 3-69). As the attacker rises upward to execute a shomen-uchi, the defender steps off the line, rotates the jo, and strikes to the rear of the leg (Figure 3-70). As the motion continues, the leg is swept out from under the attacker (Figure 3-71).

3-69

3-70   3-71

Jo against Jo

EXERCISE 1

Establish the appropriate ma-ai and ready position (Figure 3-72). As the attacker executes a tsuki with the jo, the defender pulls back slightly, raising the rear hand to execute a block (Figure 3-73). Stepping off the line of attack, the defender executes a block, a strike, and a sweep to the attacker's knee, unbalancing him (Figure 3-74).

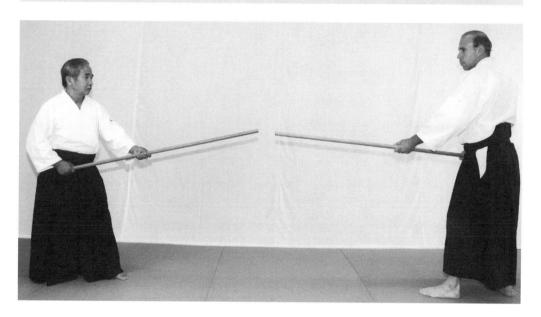

3-72

3-73

3-74

EXERCISE 2

Establish the appropriate ma-ai and ready position (Figure 3-75). As the attacker executes a tsuki with the jo, the defender pulls back slightly, raising the rear hand to execute a block (Figure 3-76). From a ready position, as an attacker approaches and begins to execute a shomen-uchi with his jo, the defender raises his rear hand defensively while sliding back slightly (Figure 3-77). As the attacker rises, the defender executes a tsuki to the throat, intercepting his attack and throwing him off balance before being touched (Figure 3-78).

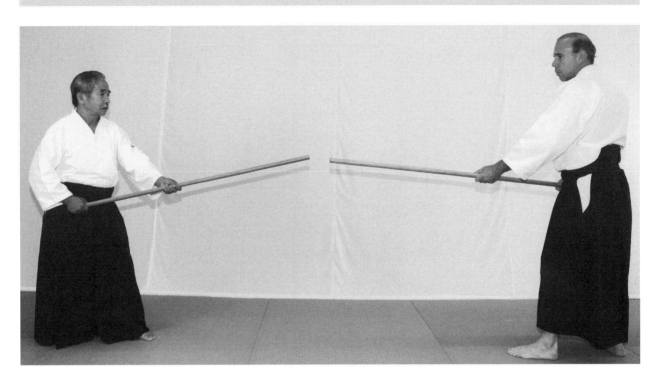

3-75

3-76

3-77

3-78

EXERCISE 3

Establish the appropriate ma-ai and ready position (Figure 3-79). As the attacker executes a tsuki with his jo, the defender slides back, raises the rear hand, and executes a low block (Figure 3-80). The attacker uses the momentum of the block to swing his jo around his head, attempting a yokomen-uchi counterstrike. The defender blends with the new attack by stepping forward, entering into and blending with the momentum and line of attack, then intercepting and capturing or controlling the hand (Figure 3-81). Following the momentum and inertia of the attack, the defender continues to pivot off the line of attack, then drops to one knee to empty the space for the attacker to fall, adding full body momentum and power to the throw (Figure 3-82).

3-79

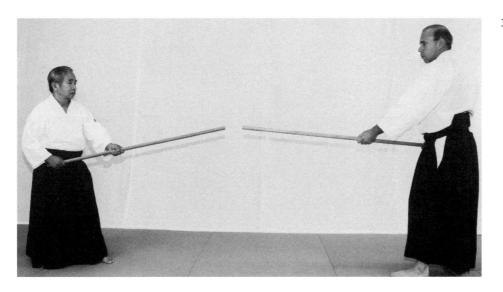

3-80

3-81

3-82

Jo against Empty Hand

EXERCISE 1

An attacker attempts a tsuki with his jo. The defender steps off the line of attack and intercepts, captures, and takes control of the jo by overextending the jo on its line of attack (Figure 3-83). Using the forward hand as a pivot point, the defender takes a tenkan circular step behind the attacker, using the jo to tie up and cross the attacker's arms (Figure 3-84) with a vertical circular motion. Following the vertical circular motion, the defender continues the momentum (Figure 3-85) into a throw (Figure 3-86).

3-83   3-84

3-85   3-86

EXERCISE 2

After an attacker has attempted a tsuki straight thrust, the defender steps off the line of attack and intercepts, captures, and controls the jo by grabbing the weapon with both hands. The defender rotates the end of the jo over the attacker's rear hand, rolling the wrist into *nikyo* (Figure 3-87). Nikyo is the second teaching or lock in which the arm is rolled over so the side of the little finger, the hand blade, is facing upward. The wrist and elbow are bent at 90-degree angles. A slight pressure downward on the elbow, while turning the hand upward, causes the joints to move in an unaccustomed direction, causing pain, compliance, and a shift in the mental focus. A slight forward push toward the rear kuzushi balance point facilitates a fall (Figures 3-88 and 3-89).

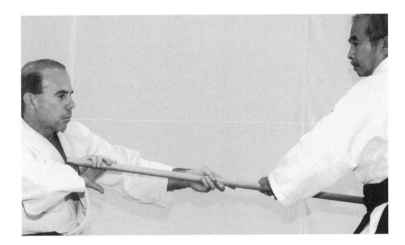

3-87

3-88

3-89

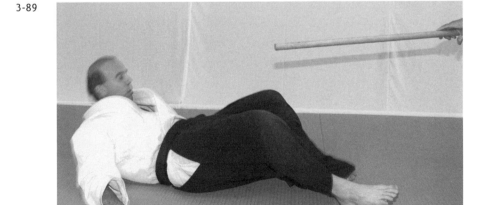

Jiyu-Waza

Practice of *jiyu-waza,* or freestyle techniques, facilitates a flowing exchange of any attack and any defense. Attempt to move slowly in rhythm, working on form, and progress in speed naturally.

Chapter 4

TANTO: WOODEN KNIFE

In feudal Japan, the tanto, or knife, was not the most important weapon. The double swords, long and short, were considered the symbol and status of the samurai. Therefore, there is little known or remaining from *tanto-jutsu-ryu*, or dagger/knife fighting styles. The availability and popularity of the knife today make training against the bladed weapon very relevant and necessary.

Selection

There are many styles and types of tanto used in practice. The two most common are the rubber and the wooden training knives. The rubber knife has the safety advantage of being flexible and relatively harmless if accidental contact is made, but the safety advantage of the rubber knife's flexibility is also a training disadvantage. The wooden knife provides a heavier feel and makes practice more realistic.

4-1: Bowing with the tanto

Blade Consciousness

Blade consciousness is very important in tanto training. Blade consciousness means always being aware and conscious of where the blade and point of the knife are. Many find it useful to place yellow tape on the blade portion of their tanto. The practitioner should never come into contact with the taped part—a touch would mean a cut. Never limit this blade consciousness to just the training and execution of techniques. All handling of the tanto should demonstrate a deep awareness and respect for the weapon's damaging and lethal potential. When attacking and slicing or stabbing, make sure the bladed edge is on the angle of attack and on target. Most real knife attacks are actually ambushes and attempted assassinations. Be very aware that the two most likely destinations after a knife fight will be the hospital and the morgue. It is better to understand that one will usually be cut during a knife fight. Then if you are cut, you are prepared. If you are not cut, all the better. To go into a knife fight expecting not to be cut is unrealistic and naive at best, fatal at worst.

Stance and Posture

The natural ready stance for tanto practice is similar to the ready stance in any practice. The body is relaxed with the spine aligned and erect. The mind is calm. The eyes maintain metsuke. The forward hand, without the tanto, is held in front of the body, directly on the centerline, in an open, receptive, but defensive, position. The rear hand, with the tanto, is held at the center, also on the centerline.

Many people like to tuck the rear hand with the tanto just behind their hip, in order to conceal the weapon. That way, the opponent does not immediately know if you have a weapon or not, and even if he is aware of the weapon, he does not know with what grip you are carrying it.

Ultimately, there is no specific stance for the tanto. One should be able to simply walk forward and attack. One should also, with consistent and persistent training, be able to defend one's self from a natural "no" stance. A no-stance is a natural ready stance that does not give any indication or signal of any offensive or defensive intent. Being neutral, one is always ready to respond spontaneously, appropriately, efficiently, and effectively.

Grip

There are four very common grips in working with a tanto. The first two are traditionally used in aikido training. They are the saber grip and the blade down grip. Two additional common grips are the reverse grip and the Filipino grip. The grip should be done with the hand, keeping the arms relaxed, placing most pressure between the base of the thumb and the last three fingers. The grip should also be relaxed and loose enough to allow and facilitate movement with the blade and switching of grips. The knife must become an extension of the arm itself.

4-2: Saber grip

The saber grip (Figure 4-2) is the most commonly practiced and used. Simply wrap your hand around the handle of the knife. The blade extends directly forward, aligned with your forearm and hand, forming a straight line. This is the same grip used with the saber sword. Holding the handle lightly with the fingers, to allow smooth and rapid movement and changes of direction, develops a great deal of sensitivity.

The blade-down grip (Figure 4-3) is commonly referred to as the "ice pick" grip. Wrap your hand around the handle with your thumb on the top of the handle.

The reverse grip is like the blade-down grip, but your wrist is rotated so that the back of the blade is held against your forearm, providing both support and concealment.

The Filipino grip is similar to the saber grip, but your thumb is placed along the top edge of the blade. Many feel that this grip makes it easier to aim the point by simply pointing the thumb.

4-3: Blade-down grip

Basic Strikes

All strikes can be, and should be, practiced from all grips. There are three basic or traditional strikes or attacks. As with the other weapons, they are the shomen-uchi, yokomen-uchi, and tsuki. Your rear leg steps forward as your rear hand, holding the weapon, strikes. The defensive hand remains on the centerline. Additionally, attacks can be thought of as having five angles, based on the clock face or the alphabet.

Shomen-Uchi

With the blade-down grip, this attack is a stab targeting the head. With a saber grip, the shomen-uchi becomes a slice or slash in a vertical plane. The angle of attack moves along a long line from the head down the centerline of the body, the full length of the torso.

4-4: Shomen-uchi

Yokomen-Uchi

With the blade-down grip, this attack is a stab targeting the side of the head and neck. With a saber grip, the yokomen-uchi becomes a slice or slash in a diagonal plane. The angle of attack moves along a long line of attack and injury.

Tsuki

The tsuki is a straight thrusting motion from the center, on the centerline, targeting the abdomen. Any of the grips

4-5: Yokomen-uchi

4-6: Tsuki

described in detail earlier can be used with any strike, slice, or thrust.

Strike Exercises

The five angles of attack are a useful model for analyzing and practicing knife training. Execute Angle 1 by attacking on the diagonal from one shoulder to the opposite hip, as in a yokomen-uchi slice. This angle becomes the first side of an X pattern. Execute Angle 2 from the other shoulder, across the body backhand, to the opposite hip, forming the other diagonal of the X. Execute Angle 3 as a horizontal attack from one hip to the other. Execute Angle 4 as the reverse or return of Angle 3, as a horizontal backhand slice across the abdomen. Execute Angle 5 as a straight thrust. Practice flowing from one angle of attack into another. Keep the attacks small and within the boundaries or gates of the body, to add to their concealment. Flow from the center or by rotating at the hips.

The clock-face pattern of practicing knife attacks is simple. Stand in a ready stance and position. A shomen-uchi strike would constitute a 12:00 o'clock downward strike, or a vertical on an angle. A yokomen-uchi strike would constitute a 3:30 strike, or a 45-degree downward angle. A tsuki would be a straight thrust into the center of the clock face. Practice attacking at all the different angles or hours. The 12:00 o'clock strike would be vertically straight down, while the 6:00 o'clock strike would be vertically straight up. The 3:00 o'clock and the 9:00 o'clock strikes would be straight horizontal strikes. The 1:00 o'clock, 2:00 o'clock, 10:00 o'clock, and 11:00 o'clock strikes follow a downward diagonal angle, while 4:00 o'clock, 5:00 o'clock, 7:00 o'clock, and 8:00 o'clock follow an upward diagonal angle.

For flexibility and creativity, practice drawing each letter of the alphabet with the blade of the tanto. You can practice writing your name or other words in the air, with the blade facing the direction of travel.

One should also practice attacking with either hand, using different and varied grips, and on different angles of attack. It is wise to practice both stabbing and slicing. In addition, one should practice using both the blade and the butt of the knife handle. For flexibility and adaptability, one can also practice both defending and attacking from standing, sitting, kneeling, and lying positions.

The Sequential Approach

The sequential approach to aikido suggests a pattern of enter and blend, redirect and unbalance, throw or control, and let go and move on. In knife fighting and defense, it is useful to think of the pattern as clear, control, and counter. Clearing the knife, or angle of attack, means getting off the line of attack, entering, and blending with the attacker. Taking control of the attack means taking charge of the momentum and inertia of the attack by further blending with it and taking charge of the weapon. Only after one is clear and in control of the weapon can a counter be safely initiated. To counter means to redirect and unbalance the attacker, throwing or controlling him, then striking atemi with various multiple slices and stabs in a reality combat situation, or performing a simple disarm in practice. Letting go should always involve zanshin and awareness of a possible renewed attack; it is wisest and safest only when the weapon has been taken away.

Knife Taking: Empty Hand against Knife

The knife was a very common weapon in feudal Japan, and is equally common on today's streets. The knife is a close-range weapon; a knife attack is initiated and defended against from a distance similar to that of empty-hand combat.

One of the best ways to become familiar with knife fighting is to learn how to attack and defend with a blade. To defend against a knife attack, one must first understand how a knife is employed. To assist your training partners in training against honest and genuine knife attacks, you must learn to use one with control and accuracy.

Learning to defend against a knife attack provides another opportunity to perfect the techniques of aikido and further condition the mind.

> **EXERCISE 1**
> The attacker initiates a tsuki thrust directly targeted to the abdomen. The defender steps off the attack line and takes control of the hand holding the tanto (Figure 4-7). The defending elbow is pointed down to prevent the bending of the elbow and to add to its intercepting and blocking power. The defender steps completely behind to the rear, turning the attacker, and beginning to unbalance him (Figure 4-8). The defender cuts the horizontal circular path of the body by executing kote-gaeshi on a vertical circular plane (Figures 4-9 and 4-10). The attacker is turned over (Figures 4-11 and 4-12) to a safe facedown position, and the knife is taken away (Figure 4-13).

4-7

4-8

4-9

4-10

4-11

4-12

4-13

EXERCISE 2
The attacker initiates a tsuki straight thrust targeting the abdomen. The defender enters by stepping off the attack line, then blends directly into the front of the attacker (Figure 4-14). Through the element of surprise, the defender captures and controls the arm without the weapon and applies an arm-entanglement lock, throwing the attacker off balance (Figure 4-15). A circular step backward forces the attacker facedown on the mat. The defender applies an arm lock to secure the attacker's submission (Figure 4-16).

4-14

4-15

4-16

EXERCISE 3

The attacker initiates a tsuki straight thrust targeting the abdomen. The defender blends backward, overextending the attacker's arm and capturing the weapon hand (Figure 4-17). While reversing direction, the defender steps forward, rotating the weapon arm upward on a vertical circular path, maintaining pressure on the elbow toward the ear and forward, to prevent a regaining of balance (Figure 4-18). While continuing the rotation, the defender steps through, applying downward pressure on the elbow and upward pressure on the wrist, *hiji-gime* (Figure 4-19). Hiji-gime is an arm-bar type of lock or pinning technique that places a great deal of torque into the locked elbow. Sliding the arm from elbow to wrist, the defender rotates the shoulder toward the kuzushi balance point and effects a knife disarm (Figure 4-20).

4-17

4-18

4-19

4-20

EXERCISE 4

The attacker approaches with a blade-down grip, executing a yokomen-uchi diagonal strike targeting the side of the neck (Figure 4-21). Blending by stepping off the line of attack and flowing with the angle of attack, the defender intercepts, not blocks, the attacking weapon hand (Figure 4-22). Allowing the attacking hand to continue on its circular path, the defender steps out of range, leaving room between the bodies for capturing and controlling the attacking hand and weapon (Figure 4-23). Rotating the center at the hip, the defender executes kote-gaeshi to throw the attacker over his own wrist (Figure 4-24).

4-21

4-22

4-23

4-24

EXERCISE 5

From a *hanmi-handachi* position (attacker standing and defender kneeling), the attacker initiates a yokomen-uchi (Figure 4-25). The defender rotates, turning from the center or hip, rises up on one leg, and intercepts—not blocks—the attacking weapon hand. Allowing the forward momentum and inertia to continue, the defender blends with the attack and begins to redirect the hand in a vertical circular path, as if executing kote-gaeshi (Figure 4-26). Removing one hand while maintaining the circular wrist turn-out pressure on the weapon hand, the defender applies pressure to the back of the knee, further breaking the attacker's balance (Figure 4-27). Continuing the pressure on both the wrist and knee, the defender stretches the attacker out, allowing him to fall and be pinned (Figure 4-28).

4-25

4-26

4-27

4-28

EXERCISE 6

From a hanmi-handachi position, the attacker initiates a tsuki straight thrust, targeting the face (Figure 4-29). The defender enters and blends by getting off the attack line and rising up on one knee to the side, then intercepts and captures the attacking hand and weapon. Following a downward vertical circular path, the defender continues the path of attack and redirects it toward the attacker's rear, while stepping through under the arm (Figure 4-30). Continuing the follow-through with momentum, the defender pulls behind the attacker and applies *sankyo* wristlock to the pressure pulse point, while removing the knife (Figure 4-31). Leading with the wrist, the defender shifts his weight forward and throws the attacker (Figure 4-32).

4-29

4-30

4-31

4-32

EXERCISE 7

From suwari-waza position (both attacker and defender kneeling), the attacker initiates a tsuki direct straight thrust, targeting the abdomen (Figure 4-33). The defender turns into and intercepts the attacking hand, applying a cross block. The defender redirects the attack on an upward vertical circular path by applying pressure to the elbow (Figure 4-34) and stepping forward into the attacker. Continuing the forward momentum, and following the vertical circular path, the defender redirects the attacker toward his front kuzushi balance point (Figure 4-35). Then, continuing the momentum facilitates a facedown pin (Figure 4-36). The hand is brought in toward the head, applying *gokyo* and disarming the attacker (Figure 4-37).

4-33

4-34

4-35

4-36

4-37

EXERCISE 8

From a suwari-waza position, the attacker initiates a tsuki targeting the abdomen (Figure 4-38). The defender moves off the line of attack to the attacker's rear, while intercepting the attacking hand and wrist with an atemi strike to the head. Following and redirecting the momentum of the attack, the defender captures and controls the attacking elbow and shoulder (Figure 4-39). Continuing the vertical circular path, the defender drives the attacker into his front kuzushi balance point from behind, until he is facedown on the mat (Figure 4-40). The defender applies a *mawashi* joint lock and disarms the attacker (Figure 4-41). Mawashi is a traditional arm-bar twisting type of pinning technique applied while the opponent or attacker is facedown on the mat or ground.

4-38

4-39

4-40

4-41

Jiyu-Waza

Freestyle practice encourages the learning of any attack and any defense.
Practice slowly at a steady pace, working on form and fluidity.

Chapter 5

ZANSHIN: A LINGERING CONNECTION

Zanshin is the lingering connection that exists long after the techniques of aikido have been executed. Zanshin is the ability to establish and maintain contact and connection. Zanshin is what you, the reader, take with you after you have finished this book. In this chapter, we present some lingering thoughts on aikido wooden weapons as a sport, and on the disadvantages and advantages of training with the three wooden weapons of aikido.

Sport

There are occasions in which knife-taking or disarming is used in a sports environment and judged on its application. This does appear to violate O'Sensei Ueshiba's injunction against aikido as a sport, but because it does exist, it is important to address the issue and be aware of it. On those occasions, the practice of weapons training, especially knife-taking, is invaluable. Also, many aikido practitioners cross-train in kendo, which has competitive tournament events.

The sports elements and application of any skill are something one should consider. Some people believe that to maintain interest and involvement in any sport, the use of a sports venue is appropriate and important. The emphasis in sport aikido is on competitive training, winning, championships, and records. Many systems of martial arts have tournaments in order to assess skill and promote visibility and participation in their art. Sporting endeavors must have built-in safeguards to prevent injuries. There are standardized criteria used to judge or score events.

While these supposedly are objective, there is no way to totally avoid sub-jectivity in the creation or application of these participation rules and judg-ing or scoring criteria.

Others feel that for maintaining combat effectiveness, the artificial rules and context of a sporting venue are inappropriate and counterpro-ductive. Safeguards of any type would not be applicable to the street or actual combat. Furthermore, the emphasis and focus on competitive win-ning are the antithesis of the spiritual values and philosophy that aikido expresses.

Disadvantages of Weapons Training

There are some disadvantages or objection to weapons training in aikido. Many of these objections are actually critiques or criticism about how to improve the weapons training practices of aikido. As with the training attack or the *uke* (attacker), the intent and intensity of the criticism may actually be the vehicle for feedback needed to improve the quality of training.

One of the objections is that training with wooden weapons takes time away from *tai-jutsu* (body art) and empty-hand training. This distinction implies that the technical, sequential, and conceptual applications of aikido are limited to what one is (or is not) holding. However, one can adopt the attitude that the same technical, sequential, and conceptual models apply to both weapons and empty-hand techniques. Therefore, the training and application remain the same, whether or not one is hold-ing something on one's hand. Given that the O'Sensei clearly states that aikido techniques come from ken-jutsu (sword arts), the practice and incorporation of weapons training may assist in the understanding and application of those techniques. There is some evidence that being able to generalize and apply the concepts from one art to another reinforces the learning process and actually reciprocally supports and validates it. Some styles of aikido, seeing the value of weapons training, insist that after an empty-hand technique is practiced, the same application must be made to the wooden weapon.

Another objection is the concern that weapons training can seduce a student away from the "true mission" of aikido, loving protection of the attacker. It is easy to see the potential to inflict more harm on the attacker with a weapon. It is because of that potential that more safeguards are learned in weapons practice, to protect the attacker from harm and show more mercy and compassion. The true goal is not doing harm or winning, for this is the opposite of aikido's goal of loving protectiveness. The goal that should be emphasized in instruction and training is the extension of that loving protection through the controlled used of the wooden weapon.

There are few instructors with weapons expertise available. Therefore, there is some danger of being taught poor weapons technique and inadequate safety measures. One should never undertake weapons training except under the curriculum and supervision of a competent instructor. The wait and search for competence is a sign of wisdom, maturity, and discipline. More instructors are realizing the importance of training with wooden weapons. More standardized curricula and certification are available.

There does appear to be some elitism or discrimination for or against those who do or don't do weapons training. Some believe that weapons training is unnecessary, while others believe it is essential. It is the blending and harmonizing of differences that make aikido. It is wise to practice not only empty-hand and weapons techniques in aikido, but also acceptance, compassion, and tolerance. There can be a tendency to fall in love with weapons training and begin to neglect one's all-around training. This provides an excellent opportunity to practice discipline in keeping one's training well rounded. Just as it is easy to neglect empty-hand techniques when working with weapons, it is equally easy to neglect the weapons when working with empty hands. Facing and confronting the egotism of elitism and discrimination help one blend and harmonize with others.

Weapons training can create a false belief that one is actually tackling a dangerous situation or conflict. This same objection can be made of empty-hand aikido training, or any martial art training. Very few systems practice in a realistic sense. By definition, all training is artificial and unrealistic. It is wise to keep that in mind. However, no training would certainly be worse than some training on how to tackle dangerous situations or conflicts. It is important to be prepared to respond appropriately to such dangers. Aikido provides that training.

Some aikido techniques are of little practical value compared to other, more combative, realistic jutsu systems. By definition, aikido is a do system, more concerned with personal and spiritual development through the practice of a martial art than with the direct application of its techniques through a jutsu, or combative fighting system. The spiritual, philosophical, and conceptual issues separate aikido from earlier styles of *aiki-jutsu*. It could equally be said that the jutsu emphasis on lethal combat techniques makes it of less practical value in everyday life, since most people will spend very little time in actual combat, and martial arts have serious legal repercussions if ever actually utilized by civilians in a street fight. The jutsu systems may be less effective in transforming or minimizing the ego, in that they may actually foster a sense of bravado and aggression. Each does what it was designed to do, and they are different in emphasis, focus, and goal. Aikido weapons training is not ken-jutsu, jo-jutsu, or tanto-jutsu. Aikido weapons training is the application and extension of aikido concepts to wooden weapons.

Weapons are too often tacked on, and not integrated into training in many styles of aikido. They deserve more attention than they receive, since they were placed in O'Sensei Morihei Ueshiba's own personal training. Others may suggest that since O'Sensei, as the founder of aikido, did not emphasize them at the Hombu Dojo, they were afterthoughts and were not to be given equal status or time.

Technically, wooden weapons are reproductions of once-lethal weapons and are illegal to carry in today's society. This objection or criticism focuses on the weapon, not on the application of aikido concepts through training. One would not want to train with a lethal weapon for fear of accidents. The wood, then and now, provides a means to practice relatively safely and inexpensively. The replication reflects the time and culture from which aikido evolved. Most weapons are illegal to carry; check your local jurisdiction for exact restrictions, limits, and penalties. The fact that they are illegal as weapons supports the evidence that even wooden weapons can be dangerous, especially in the hands of an untrained individual with ill intent.

Finally, too often, weapons training is simply learned by rote or memorized as mechanical techniques, without a true understanding and integration of aikido concepts. This can lead to sloppy solo training and engrain bad techniques and mechanics, such as the tendency to use a weapon for power instead of relying on one's own body mechanics. As mentioned, because there are so few who practice weapons aikido as a specialty, the curriculum may become somewhat diluted. It may be wiser to seek outside training. This disadvantage or constructive criticism reinforces the need to train with weapons to the point that it may not be a specialty, but is an integrated and integral part of aikido training. Training should focus on the understanding and integration of such aikido concepts as proper posture, position, and mechanics. Many people supplement their aikido weapons training by also cross-training in other weapons arts, such as ken-jutsu or kendo, iai-jutsu or iai-do, or jo-jutsu or jodo.

Benefits of Weapons Training

There are many benefits to studying weapons techniques as an integrated and integral part of aikido training. O'Sensei Morihei Ueshiba extensively trained with weapons and stressed that the physical aikido techniques came from the sword art.

Weapons naturally extend the reach. This extension means that training with wooden weapons helps develop a sense of distance, or ma-ai. This is one of the benefits of training with weapons—it forces one to consider the range or distance that the weapon makes available. It is always important to stay outside the range of power, or to enter and blend inside the range of power to neutralize the attack. Ma-ai awareness, consciousness, and responsiveness are essential for training in empty-hand martial arts, but are equally essential to training with weapons.

Training with wooden weapons helps develop a sense of ki extension. As one develops in aikido training through consistent and persistent training, one begins to think beyond the physical technique. As was seen in the initial discussion on ki training, the ability to extend ki is important. The use of a weapon provides a means to think past the hands and learn to extend ki into the weapon. One of the best ways to think about this aspect of weapons training is to feel and think of the weapon as an extension of the self, and as something that is "one with" the body. The body alignment of shoulder, elbow, and hand extends into the weapon. By focusing on controlling the tip of the weapon, one builds an internal kinesthetic or feeling sense of the tip of the weapon as an extension of the body and of the ki flow.

Weapons extend the power possible to inflict harm and damage. Therefore, this potential necessitates that one learn even more control of a technique. As stated, all empty-hand techniques can be executed or performed with the weapons. The difference is that an empty-hand atemi will produce the possibility of some harm and injury, while the same strike delivered with the momentum and inertia of a wooden sword, stick, or knife can be forceful and powerful enough to cause devastating damage or death. Weapons training helps teach students the potential of their power and the necessity for self-control. True compassion and mercy come from having the ability and opportunity to do harm, but not following through, as a result of training, self-restraint, and concern. Human life is very fragile and precious—one must realize this. Weapons training can help one develop that deeper appreciation for human life and the need to protect it, even from oneself. Weapons training assists one in the realization, immediate awareness, and understanding that even in training there is a high risk of potential harm and injury. Aikido, even as applied using weapons, is for the protection of life, even when one is capable of inflicting lethal damage with weapons.

No training will provide a better opportunity to focus on an attack and timing than weapons training. The necessity of perceiving the path or line of attack and responding with appropriate timing becomes more crucial in weapons training.

Training with traditional, though wooden, weapons involves the student in the cultural heritage and history of aikido. It keeps one in touch with Japanese culture and tradition. The traditional and social aspects of training with wooden weapons help maintain a cultural identity that ties aikido back to budo and *bujutsu*. Weapons training, like empty-hand training, must always maintain the very traditional formal aspect of etiquette.

Training with wooden weapons can give the practitioner an edge over others who do not practice or train with and against weapons. There is a different level of intent and intensity to weapons training. Training with wooden weapons helps overcome the fear of weapons encounters. The increased danger equals the increase in the development of that fighting edge. It extends and expands the feeling of effectiveness and efficiency with additional variety and validation. It develops and increases the awareness and appreciation of the advantage weapons give—even for the bad guys. If the defender lacks this awareness, training, and discipline, it is only the bad guy who has the advantage. The best way to defeat a weapon is to know how it is used.

Weapons training allows the student the opportunity to perceive and practice the techniques and concepts of aikido beyond empty hands and into every aspect of training. The application of the concepts and principles of empty-hand aikido techniques to weapons training assists and promotes the generalization of the learning experience. Training with a variety of weapons, as well as empty hands, facilitates the student's ability to adapt, adjust, and improvise. Weapons training expands, complements, and supplements—but never replaces—training with empty hands, especially when empty-hand techniques are used against weapons. Weapons training helps improve the body mechanics necessary for balance, using the hips, footwork, distancing, timing, and strength. Weapons training can make the spiral circular movements within a technique clearer. Weapons training demands a coordination of body, timing, and distance. Training brings improvement in ma-ai, rhythm, timing, *sabaki* (body motion), and kuzushi. The use and benefits of incorporating the atemi are easily recognized. Weapons training promotes zanshin concentration and awareness because mistakes are obvious and require one to focus on the safety of the opponent or training partner.

Weapons training provides a means of solo practice through visualizing an imaginary opponent. This use of imagination and mental focus actually aids in improving a sense of body consciousness. Solo practice helps promote health and self-defense skills. Weapons training can be enjoyed by older practitioners who are losing strength or have incurred injuries, to help prevent the loss of skills and conditioning.

Aikido is budo. The goal of aikido is the development of personal, social, and spiritual awareness, responsibility, and accountability through the discipline and practice of a martial art. Aikido, empty-handed and with weapons, is the training of the heart and mind for self-defense, if necessary, and for physical conditioning.

The three steps of budo training are *shu* to preserve form, *ha* to break form, and *ri* to separate from form. Aikido weapons training and techniques are a means to practice misogi, or purification rituals and disciplines. Aikido views victory over the self as more important than victory over an opponent. Therefore, through aikido weapons training and practice, one learns to view one's self as the true target, as one's biggest and fiercest opponent. Mentally, the training in aikido weapons conditions the mind to try new things and to expand the application of aikido concepts. Learning to hold the wooden weapon gently but firmly is likened to holding life in one's hand. Training in aikido wooden weapons is thus training for personal, social, and spiritual development.

Besides the practical and esoteric aspects and values of weapons training, it is an enjoyable experience. The best way to reach, or surpass, a destination is simply to enjoy the journey.

GLOSSARY

The words and phrases listed in this glossary are commonly used in weapons training and are heard in the dojo.

Ai: Harmony

Aiki: United, blending, or harmonizing with spirit

Aikido: The way of harmonizing energy or spirit

Aiki drop: A no-touch throw performed by dropping down, emptying space

Aiki-jo: The five-foot or less stick/staff used in aikido, usually associated with Saito Sensei

Aiki-jujitsu, aiki-jutsu: Styles of martial arts that emphasize aiki and fighting

Aiki-ken: The wooden sword used in aikido, usually associated with Saito Sensei

Aiki-otoshi-nage: A throw performed by picking up the training partner's legs

"Arigato": "Thank you" (informal)

Ashi-sabaki: Footwork

Atemi: Strike to a vital point

Ato: Move back

Awase: Blend

Bo: A wooden staff over five feet in length

Bo-jutsu: Wooden staff fighting

Boken: A wooden sword, commonly referred to as a ken

Budo: The martial way

Bugei: An early word for combative martial arts

Buki-waza: Weapons techniques

Bushi: An early term for a samurai

Bushido: The way and code of the warrior

Chinkon: A calming tranquility of the soul

Chudan: The middle position, with the weapon held horizontally

Chudan-zuki: Punch to the abdomen

Daito-ryu: A martial art that influenced aikido

Dan: Black-belt ranks

Do: Way

Dogi: The training uniform

Dojo: The training hall or school, the "way (do) place"

Dojo-cho: The leader or head of the dojo

"Domo": "Thanks" (informal)

"Domo-arigato": "Thank you" (formal)

"Domo-arigato-gozaimashita": "Thank you very much" (past tense, spoken after receiving instruction or after class)

"Domo-arigato-gozaimasu": "Thank you very much" (very formal, present tense, spoken while receiving instruction or during class)

Doshu: The head or keeper of the way

"Dozo": "Please, go ahead" (spoken politely in the dojo while training, regarding allowing another to go ahead)

Gedan: The low position, with the weapon held point-downward

Gedan-zuki: Downward punch

Geikikan-jutsu: Ball-and-chain fighting

Geri: Kick

Gi: Short for dogi, training uniform

Giri: Duty

Godan: Fifth-degree black belt

Gokyo: The fifth pinning technique

"Gomen-nasai": "Excuse me; I'm sorry" (spoken in the dojo to acknowledge a mistake or error)

Gono-sen: An immediate response, counterattack

Gyaku: Reverse, opposite, inverted

Gyaku-hanmi: Reverse posture

Gyaku-uchi: A reverse strike

Gyaku-zuki: Punching with rear the hand, cross

Ha: A stage of learning breaking from form, or a variation

Hachidan: Eighth-degree black belt

"Hai": "Yes" (spoken in the dojo to express acknowledgment or agreement)

"Hajime": "Start" (spoken in the dojo as an order to begin practice)

Hakama: Traditional pleated split-legged skirt or pants

Hanmi: The half-forward stance; oblique stance

Hanmi-handachi: A position with the attacker standing and the defender kneeling or seated

Happo-baraki: To be totally aware of one's surroundings

Hara: The abdomen, stomach, center

"Hayaku": "Quickly" (spoken in the dojo to expedite training)

Henka-waza: Variation techniques

Hidari: Left

Hiji: Elbow

Hiji-dori: The elbow grab

Hiji-gime: The elbow/arm bar

Hitoemi: A stance in which neither foot is forward or back, but equally parallel

Hombu Dojo: The home or headquarters school

Iai-do: Sword drawing

Iai-goshi: A stance with the hips lowered in stable position

Iai-jutsu: The defensive sword-drawing fighting style

"Iie": "No" (spoken in the dojo to acknowledge lack of understanding or disagreement)

Ikkyo: The first pinning technique

Irimi: Entering

Irimi-nage: An entering throw

Irimi-tenkan: Entering and turning

Iwama-ryu: The school in Iwama, Japan, under Saito Sensei, with an emphasis on weapons training

Jiyu-waza: Freestyle techniques

Jo: A short stick or staff

Jo-jutsu: Short stick/staff fighting

Jodan: The upper position, with the weapon held pointing upward or above the head

Jodan-zuki: An upper strike

Judan: Tenth-degree black belt

Juji-nage: A cross-arms throw

Juken: The bayonet and rifle

Juken-jutsu: Bayonet fighting

Junbi-taiso: Warmup exercises

Jutsu: A combative fighting system

Jutte-jutsu: Metal truncheon fighting

Kaeshi: A counter or reversal

Kaeshi-waza: Countering techniques

Kaeshi-zuki: A counterthrust

Kaiten: Rotation

Kaiten-nage: A rotary throw

Kamae: A posture, stance

Kami/kamisama: Spirit/spirits

Kan: Intuition

Kashima Shinto-ryu ken-jutsu: An offshoot of the Katori Shinto-ryu, influential on aiki-ken

Kata: A prearranged practice form or pattern

Kata-dori: A shoulder hold

Katate-dori: Held by one hand

Katate-uchi: A one-handed strike

Katori Shinto-ryu ken-jutsu: An early sword-fighting school

Keiko: Training/practice

Kendo: Sword sport

Ken-jutsu: Offensive sword fighting

Ki: Vital energy

Kihon: Fundamental

"Kiyotsukete": "Be careful" (imperative)

Kiza: Kneeling on the toes

Kohai: A junior student

Kokoichi: A concept, situation, and training level in which defense and offense blend

Kokyu: Animated breathing

Kokyu-dosa: Breath power movement; exercise; a technique performed from a kneeling position

Kokyu-ho: A turning step with breathing and ki extension

Kokyu-nage: A breath, or timing, throw

Kosa-dori: A hand grab

Koshi: Hip

Koshiita: The back panel of the hakama

Koshi-nage: A hip throw

Koshukai: Lecture classes

Kote: Wrist

Kote-gaeshi-nage: A wrist turn-out throw

Koutai: Change

Kubi: Neck

Kubishime: Chokes

Kudan: Ninth-degree black belt

Kuzushi: Balance breaking

Kyu: Ranks below black belt

Kyu-jutsu: Bow-and-arrow fighting

Ma-ai: Distance

Mae: Forward

"Mate": "Wait" (spoken in the dojo to order or request a stop or pause)

Mawashi: A ground-pinning arm bar; to turn; a rotation

"Mawatte": "Turn around" (Spoken in the dojo to order or request an about-face)

Men: Head

Men-uchi: A strike to the head

Metsuke: Soft eye focus

Migi: Right

Misogi: Purification rituals or practices

Mokuso: Closed-eye meditation

Morote: Both hands

Morote-dori: Two hands grabbing one hand

Mudansha: Kyu ranks, lower than black-belt ranks

Mune: Chest

Mune-dori: A one- or two-hand lapel hold

Mune-tsuki: An abdominal strike to the belt knot

Mushin: Empty (mu) mind (shin)

Musubi: Connection

Nagashi: Flow

Nagashi-waza: Flowing or combination techniques

Nage: A throw, to throw, or the person doing the throwing technique

Nage-waza: Throwing techniques

Nanadan: Seventh-degree black belt

Nidan: Second-degree back belt

Nikyo: The second pinning technique

Obi: Belt

Oi-zuki: A step punch

Omote: Entering to the front

Omoto: A Shinto religious cult that influenced O'Sensei Morihei Ueshiba

"Onegaishimasu": "Please" (spoken in the dojo to request or ask for something politely)

O'Sensei: Great teacher, referring to Morihei Ueshiba

Otagai-ni-rei: To bow to each other

Otoshi: To drop

Randori: Training with multiple fellow students or a training partner

Rei: Bowing

Reigi: Etiquette

Renshu: Hard work on basics

Ri: The stage of budo training that separates from form

Rokkyo: The sixth pinning or control technique, *hiji-kime-osae* is an arm-bar type of technique applying pressure to the extended elbow

Rokudan: Sixth-degree black belt

Ronin: A samurai without a master

Ryokata-dori: Grabbing both shoulders

Ryote-dori: Both hands grasping both hands

Sabaki: Body motion

Samurai: To serve; a Japanese feudal warrior in service to a master

Sandan: Third-degree black belt

Sankyo: The third pinning technique

Sasumata-jutsu: Forked-staff fighting

Seidan: A position in which the weapon is held pointing toward the eyes

Seiza: A sitting posture, kneeling on both calves

Sempai: Senior student; higher rank

Sen: A response initiated after analysis of the opponent's position

Sen-no-sen: Initiating a response upon perceiving the opponent's intent

Sensei: Teacher/instructor

Sensei-ni-rei: A bow to the teacher/instructor

Shihan: A master teacher

Shiho-nage: The four-direction throw

Shinai: A split-bamboo sword

Shikko: Knee-walking, moving on one's knees

Shinshin: Mind and body

Shinto: A religion that believes in spirits, nature, and ancestor worship, very influential on O'Sensei Morihei Ueshiba

Shinzen-ni-rei: A bow to a shrine

Shodan: First-degree black belt

Shomen: Face/head; straight ahead

Shomen-uchi: A frontal downward head strike

Shoshin: Beginner's mind

Shu: The stage of learning that preserves form (kata)

Shugyo: Rigorous daily training, pursuit of knowledge

Shuriken-jutsu: Blade-throwing fighting

Shuto: The edge of the hand

Sode: Sleeve

Sode-dori: A sleeve grab

Sodegarami-jutsu: Barbed-pole fighting

So-jutsu: Spear fighting

Soke: The head of a family system or style

Soto: Outside

"Sumimasen": "Excuse me" (said to attract attention)

Suwari-waza: Seated techniques

Suwatte: To sit down

Tachi: Standing

Tachi-waza: Standing techniques

Taisabaki: Body turning

Takemusu-aiki: The spontaneous execution of an aikido technique

Tanden: The abdomen, stomach, center, hara

Tatami: The traditional Japanese floor mat, made of rice straw

Tatte: To raise

Te-gatana: A hand-blade

Tenbin-nage: An elbow-lock throw

Tenkan: Circular-pivoting footwork

Tenkai: Step and pivot, a sweeping body turn

Tenshin: Heaven and earth

Tenshinkai: Name given by O'Sensei Morihei Ueshiba to the flowing and powerful style of aikido from Vietnam, meaning "from the association of heavenly hearts," or "organization of heaven on earth." This style and organization is headed by Phong Thong Dang

Tenshin-nage: The heaven-and-earth throw

Tenugui: A small hand-cloth

Tessen-jutsu: Iron-fan fighting

Tetsubo-jutsu: Iron-bar fighting

Tohai: Of the same rank

Tori: The person defending

Tsugi-ashi: Lunge or shuffle footwork

Tsuki: Punch

Uchi: Strike, inside

Uchi-deshi: A live-in student

Uke: The training partner who receives the technique, the attacker

Ukemi: Falling ways, receiving techniques with the body

Ura: Turning to the rear, back

Ushiro: From the rear, behind

Ushiro-eri-dori: A neck/collar grab from the rear

Ushiro-kubi-shime: A choke from the rear

Ushiro-ryote-dori: Grabbing both wrists from the rear

Ushiro-ryote kata-dori: Grabbing both shoulders from the rear

Ushiro-tekubi-dori: A wrist grab from the rear

Ushiro-udoroshi: Pulled down from behind

"Wakarimasu": "I understand"

Waza: Technique

Yame: Stop

Yodan: Fourth-degree black belt

"Yoi": "Ready" (spoken in the dojo to indicate preparedness)

Yoko: Horizontal; to the side

Yokomen-uchi: A diagonal strike to the head or neck

Yoko-uchi: A sideward strike

Yonkyo: The fourth pinning technique

Yudansha: Members of dan black-belt rank

Yukuri: Slow

Yuru-yaka-ni: Smooth

Zanshin: Lingering mind, spirit, or connection

Zenpo: Front

Zori: Japanese sandals worn outside the dojo

REFERENCES, RESOURCES, AND RECOMMENDATIONS

Books

Babin, Richard W. *Iaido Sword: Kamimoto-Ha Techniques of Muso Shinden Ryu.* Boulder, Colorado: Paladin Press, 2003.

Craig, Darrel Max. *Iai: The Art of Drawing the Sword.* Tokyo: Lotus Press, 1985.

—————. *The Heart of Kendo.* Boston, Massachusetts: Shambhala Publications, Inc., 1999.

Dang, Phong Thong and Lynn Seiser.. *Advanced Aikido.* Boston, Massachusetts: Tuttle Publishing, 2005.

—————. *Aikido Basics.* Boston, Massachusetts: Tuttle Publishing, 2003.

Dang, Tri Thong. *Beyond the Known: The Ultimate Goal of the Martial Arts.* Boston, Massachusetts: Tuttle Publishing, 1993.

—————. *Toward the Unknown: Martial Artist, What Shall You Become?* Boston, Massachusetts: Tuttle Publishing, 1997.

Draeger, Donn F. and Robert W. Smith. *Asian Fighting Arts.* Tokyo: Kodansha International, 1969.

Draeger, Donn F. *Classical Budo: The Martial Arts and Ways of Japan, Volume Two.* New York: Weatherhill, Inc., 1973.

—————. *Classical Bujutsu: The Martial Arts and Ways of Japan, Volume One.* Trumbull, Connecticut: Weatherhill, Inc., 1973.

Finn, Michael. *Iaido: The Way of the Sword.* London: Paul H. Crompton Ltd., 1982.

Heckler, Richard Strozzi. *Aikido and the New Warrior.* Berkeley, California: North Atlantic Books, 1985.

—————. *The Anatomy of Change: A Way to Move Through Life's Transitions.* Berkeley, California: North Atlantic Books, 1984.

—————. *In Search of the Warrior Spirit: Teaching Awareness Disciplines to the Green Berets.* Berkeley, California: North Atlantic Books, 1990.

Homma, Gaku. *The Structure of Aikido, Volume 1: Kenjutsu & Taijutsu Sword and Open-hand Movement Relationships.* Berkeley, California: Frog, Ltd., 1997.

Kiyota, Minoru. *The Shambhala Guide to Kendo.* Boston, Massachusetts: Shambhala Publications, Inc., 1995.

Lowry, Dave. *Bokken: Arts of the Japanese Sword.* Santa Clarita, California: Ohara Publications, 1986.

———. *Jo: Art of the Japanese Short Staff.* Santa Clarita, California: Ohara Publications, 1987.

Musashi, Miyamoto. Thomas Cleary, trans. *The Book of Five Rings.* Boston, Massachusetts: Shambhala Publications, Inc., 1994.

Perry, Susan. *Remembering O'Sensei.* Boston, Massachusetts: Shambhala Publications, Inc., 2002.

Pranin, Stanley. *The Aiki News Encyclopedia of Aikido.* Tokyo: Aiki News, 1991.

———. *Aikido Journal/Aiki News Complete Archives.* Las Vegas, Nevada: Aikido Journal, 2004.

Random, Michael. *The Martial Arts.* London: Peerage Books/Octopus Books Ltd., 1977.

Saotome, Mitsugi. *Aikido and the Harmony of Nature.* Boston, Massachusetts: Shambhala Publications, Inc., 1986.

Sasamori, Junzo and Gordon Warner. *This Is Kendo: The Art of Japanese Fencing.* Tokyo: Charles E. Tuttle Co., Inc., 1964.

Shifflett, C. M. *Ki in Aikido: A Sampler of Ki Exercises.* Merrifield, Virginia: Round Earth Publishing, 1997.

———. *Aikido: Exercises for Teaching and Training.* Merrifield, Virginia: Round Earth Publishing, 1999.

Stevens, John. *Aikido: The Way of Harmony.* Boston, Massachusetts: Shambhala Publications, Inc., 1984.

———. *The Art of Peace.* Boston, Massachusetts: Shambhala Publications, Inc., 1992.

———. *Budo Secrets: Teaching of the Martial Arts Masters.* Boston, Massachusetts: Shambhala Publications, Inc., 2001.

———. *Invincible Warrior: A Pictorial Biography of Morihei Ueshiba, the Founder of Aikido.* Boston, Massachusetts: Shambhala Publications, Inc., 1997.

———. *The Secrets of Aikido.* Boston, Massachusetts: Shambhala Publications, Inc., 1995.

———. *The Shambhala Guide to Aikido.* Boston, Massachusetts: Shambhala Publications, Inc., 1996.

Stevens, John and Walther V. Krenner. *Training with the Master: Lessons with Morihei Ueshiba, Founder of Aikido*. Boston, Massachusetts: Shambhala Publications, Inc., 1999.

Tohei, Koichi. *Aikido: The Coordination of Mind and Body for Self-defense*. Tokyo: Rikugei Publishing House, 1961.

————. *Aikido in Daily Life*. Tokyo: Rikugei Publishing House, 1966.

————. *Book of Ki: Co-ordinating Mind and Body in Daily Life*. Tokyo: Japan Publishing Trading Co., 1976.

————. *Ki in Daily Life*. Tokyo: Japan Publishing Trading Co., 1978.

————. *Ki No Shu Ren Ho: How to Develop Ki*. Tokyo: Ki No Kenyukai HQ, 1973.

Tsunetomo, Yamamoto. *Hagakure: The Book of the Samurai*. New York: Kodansha International, 1979.

Ueshiba, Kisshomaru. *Aikido*. Tokyo: Hozansha Publishing, 1972.

————. *The Spirit of Aikido*. Tokyo: Kodansha International, 1984.

Ueshiba, Kisshomaru and Moriteru Ueshiba. *Best Aikido: The Fundamentals*. Tokyo: Kodansha International, 2002.

Ueshiba, Morihei. *Budo Teachings of the Founder of Aikido*. Tokyo: Kodansha International, 1991.

————. *Budo Training in Aikido*. Tokyo: Sugawara Martial Arts Institute/Japan Publications, 1997.

Ueshiba, Moriteru. *The Aikido Master Course Best Aikido 2*. Tokyo: Kodansha International, 2003.

Westbrook, A. and O. Ratti. *Aikido and the Dynamic Sphere*. Rutland, Vermont: Charles E. Tuttle Company, 1970.

————. *Secrets of the Samurai: The Martial Arts of Feudal Japan*. Rutland, Vermont: Charles E. Tuttle Company, 1973.

Williams, Bryn. *Martial Arts of the Orient*. New York: Hamlyn Publishing Group, 1975.

Zier, Don and Tom Lang. *Jo: The Japanese Short Staff*. Burbank, California: Unique Publications, Inc., 1985.

Magazines

Aikido Today Magazine. Susan Perry, Editor. Arete Press
    (1420 N. Claremont Blvd., #204C-D, Claremont, CA 91711).
    No longer in paper publication.

DVDs

Guerri, Patricia. *Iwama-Ryu Aikido.* Palaiseau, France: Independence
    Productions, 2005.

Saito, Morihiro. *Aiki Ken.* DVD. Las Vegas, Nevada: *Aikido Journal,* 2003.

———. *Aiki Jo.* DVD. Las Vegas, Nevada: *Aikido Journal,* 2003.

Internet Articles and Forums

www.AikidoJournal.com (This is the paperless former *Aiki-News* and *Aikido
Journal.*)

www.AikiWeb.com

ABOUT THE AUTHORS

Sensei Phong Thong Dang holds a ryokuba (sixth-degree black belt) in aikido, a sixth dan in tae kwon do, a fifth dan in judo, and an eighth dan in Vietnamese Shaolin kung fu. The World Martial Arts Hall of Fame inducted Phong Sensei twice, once for his expertise in aikido and again for his lifelong dedication to the martial arts for over fifty years. Phong Sensei received his third-degree black belt/sandan directly from the Aikikai Hombu Dojo and aikido founder O'Sensei Morihei Ueshiba and his son Doshu Kisshomaru Ueshiba. O'Sensei Morihei Ueshiba gave the name Tenshinkai, meaning "from the association of heavenly hearts" or "heaven on earth," to the unique flowing and powerful style of aikido from Vietnam. O'Sensei Morihei Ueshiba personally gave the honor and responsibility of spreading Tenshinkai aikido directly to Phong Sensei. Phong Sensei has been featured in *Aikido Today Magazine, Aikido Journal, Karate Illustrated, Martial Arts and Combat Sports, Arts Martiaux Traditionnels d'Asie,* and *Black Belt* magazine. Phong Sensei teaches daily at the Westminster Aikikai Dojo, headquarters and home school of the International Tenshinkai Aikido Federation, in Westminster, California, USA.

Lynn Seiser, Ph.D., MFT, is a perpetual student of the martial arts. He has trained for over thirty-five years in various forms of martial arts and fighting systems, including military H2H/CQC. Currently he studies and holds sandan (third-degree black-belt) rank in Tenshinkai aikido under Phong Sensei at the Westminster Aikikai Dojo in Westminster, California. Dr. Seiser has a bachelor's degree in psychology and philosophy, a master's degree in marriage, family, and child counseling, and a doctorate in psychology. Dr. Seiser is an internationally respected psychotherapist and marriage, family, and child counselor, with over twenty-five years of direct clinical experience in the treatment of perpetrators and victims of violence, trauma, abuse, and addiction. Dr. Seiser has coauthored several books in martial arts and clinical psychotherapy interventions and techniques, and a chapter on mental imagery and visualization in sport psychology. He has regular Southern California columns in a local newspaper and magazine. His work has appeared in *Black Belt* magazine, *Martial, Martial Arts and Combat Sports,* and *Aikido Today Magazine.* Dr. Seiser founded Aiki-Solutions to provide consultation and training in sport and performance psychology and conflict awareness, assessment, prevention, management, and resolution.

MORE BOOKS FROM THE
TUTTLE MARTIAL ARTS LIBRARY

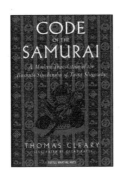

CODE OF THE SAMURAI
A Modern Translation of the Bushido Shoshinshu of Taira Shigesuke
by Thomas Cleary
5 X 7 ½, 128 pp., Hardcover, $14.95
ISBN-10: 0-8048-3190-4
ISBN-13: 978-0-8048-3190-1

A powerful contemporary translation of the classic treatise of the Way of the Warrior—still the core of Japanese social, political, and corporate structure—as compelling now as when it was first written 400 years ago.

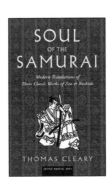

SOUL OF THE SAMURAI
Modern Translations of Three Classic Works of Zen and Bushido
by Thomas Cleary
5 X 7 ½, 160 pp., Hardcover, $14.95
ISBN-10: 0-8048-3690-6
ISBN-13: 978-0-8048-3690-6

This modern translation of three classics of martial arts philosophy reveals the powerful influence of Zen—and captures the true soul of the samurai.

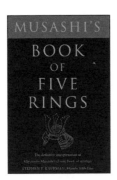

MUSASHI'S BOOK OF FIVE RINGS
The Definitive Interpretation of Miyamoto Musashi's Classic Book of Strategy
by Stephen F. Kaufman
5 ½ X 8 ½, 128 pp., Paperback, $13.95
ISBN-10: 0-8048-3520-9
ISBN-13: 978-0-8048-3520-6

A definitive treatise on mortal combat from one of Japan's most formidable warriors—the martial arts luminary Miyamoto Musashi.

SAMURAI STRATEGIES
42 Martial Secrets from Musashi's Book of Five Rings
by Boyé Lafayette De Mente
5 ¼ X 8, 128 pp., Paperback, $12.95
ISBN-10: 0-8048-3683-3
ISBN-13: 978-0-8048-3683-8

17th-century strategies full of valuable insights for anyone in any field of endeavor—from business, war, and sports to art, love, and politics.